Committees, Agendas, and Voting

FUNDAMENTALS OF PURE AND APPLIED ECONOMICS

ADVISORY BOARD

Fundamentals of Pure and Applied Economics is an international series of titles divided by discipline into sections. A list of sections and their editors and of published titles may be found at the back of this volume.

Committees, Agendas, and Voting

Nicholas R. Miller
University of Maryland Baltimore County, USA

A volume in the Political Science and Economics section

edited by

J. Ferejohn
Stanford University, California, USA

Routledge
Taylor & Francis Group
LONDON AND NEW YORK

First Published 1995 by Harwood Academic Publishers.

Published 2004 by Routledge
4 Park Square, Milton Park, Abingdon, Oxon OX14 4RN
605 Third Avenue, New York, NY 10017

Routledge is an imprint of the Taylor & Francis Group, an informa business

Library of Congress Cataloging-in-Publication Data

Miller, Nicholas R., 1941–
    Committees, agendas, and voting / Nicholas R. Miller.
      p.   cm. -- (Fundamentals of pure and applied economics, ISSN
0191-1708 ; v. Political science and economics section)
    Includes bibliographical references (p.   ).
    ISBN 3-7186-5569-1
    1. Social choice--Mathematical models. 2. Voting--Mathematical
models. 3. Committees--Mathematical models. I. Title.
II. Series: Fundamentals of pure and applied economics ; v.
III. Series: Fundamentals of pure and applied economics. Political
science and economics section.
HB846.8.M54 1995
302'.13--dc20
                             94-6282
                             CIP

ISBN 13: 978-3-7186-5569-4 (pbk)

Contents

Introduction to the Series

Drawing on a personal network, an economist can still relatively easily stay well informed in the narrow field in which he works, but to keep up with the development of economics as a whole is a much more formidable challenge. Economists are confronted with difficulties associated with the rapid development of their discipline. There is a risk of 'balkanization' in economics, which may not be favorable to its development.

Fundamentals of Pure and Applied Economics has been created to meet this problem. The discipline of economics has been subdivided into sections (listed at the back of this volume). These sections comprise short books, each surveying the state of the art in a given area.

Each book starts with the basic elements and goes as far as the most advanced results. Each should be useful to professors needing material for lectures, to graduate students looking for a global view of a particular subject, to professional economists wishing to keep up with the development of their science, and to researchers seeking convenient information on questions that incidentally appear in their work.

Each book is thus a presentation of the state of the art in a particular field rather than a step-by-step analysis of the development of the literature. Each is a high-level presentation but accessible to anyone with a solid background in economics, whether engaged in business, government, international organizations, teaching, or research in related fields.

Three aspects of *Fundamentals of Pure and Applied Economics* should be emphasized:

- First, the project covers the whole field of economics, not only theoretical or mathematical economics.
- Second, the project is open-ended and the number of books is not predetermined. If new and interesting areas appear, they will generate additional books.
- Last, all the books making up each section will later be grouped to constitute one or several volumes of an Encyclopedia of Economics.

The editors of the sections are outstanding economists who have selected as authors for the series some of the finest specialists in the world.

To the memory of
Duncan Black
1908–1991

Committees, Agendas, and Voting*

NICHOLAS R. MILLER

University of Maryland Baltimore County, USA

1. COMMITTEE VOTING

What happens when a group of individuals must collectively choose by means of voting, one alternative out of a larger set alternatives, concerning which they may have conflicting preferences? This is the *voting problem*. Here we focus more specifically on *committee voting* – that is, voting in a parliamentary context, in which collective choice proceeds through a sequence of *binary* (e.g., yes/no) votes.

In the event that three or more alternatives are under consideration, the voting problem turns out to be fraught with a variety of complexities. Because of these complexities, and because at the same time voting is a common phenomenon used by groups ranging from small committees to mass electorates, an extensive theoretical literature has developed on the subject. And because the voting problem entails matters of rational individual and group choice, and of strategy and coalition formation, this theoretical literature has developed primarily within the framework of economic theory, game theory, and social choice theory. The purpose of this essay is to survey the concepts, analytical techniques, and results of that portion of this literature that deals specifically with committee voting.

*This research was supported in part by NSF Grant SES-85-09680 and by a Designated Research Initiative Fund Grant from the University of Maryland Graduate School, Baltimore. I thank Steven Brams, John Ferejohn, Richard McKelvey, Jack Nagel, and Hannu Nurmi for helpful comments and corrections. No doubt errors remain, for which the author is responsible.

1

The theory of voting has its origins in the work of such enlightenment philosophers and mathematicians as Borda, Condorcet, and Laplace, and it was further developed some hundred years later by C. L. Dodgson, better known as Lewis Carroll. Little further progress was made until nearly fifty years ago when the British economist Duncan Black wrote a series of articles (most notably, Black, 1948) on the logic of committees and elections, which he later consolidated into a book on *The Theory of Committees and Elections* (1958). Black's work focused on committee voting, with some extensions to elections more generally. Here is how Black (1958: pp. 1–2) described the scope of his work.

> The present book will present the logic of committee decisions.... By a *committee* we will mean any group of people who arrive at a decision by means of voting.... The theory will ... be developed in relation to a committee which is choosing one out of the various motions which are put forward on a particular topic. A *motion* we define as any proposal before a committee which it may adopt or reject by a method of voting. It is accepted practice that the motions between which a vote is taken should propose a course of action which are alternative to one another....

Since Black revived the subject, many economists and political scientists, as well as some philosophers, mathematicians, and others, have made important contributions to the theory of committee voting, which has evolved in a cumulative fashion. The most notable single contribution was Robin Farquharson's *Theory of Voting* (1969a), which explicitly addressed the strategic and game-theoretic aspect of voting that Black largely sidestepped. An equally important general contribution has been the development of the so-called 'spatial theory of voting,' in which the set of alternatives is taken to be a space of one or more dimensions. Finally, the theory of voting has to some extent been subsumed by the more abstract and comprehensive *theory of social choice* originated by Arrow (1951). But we focus here on committee voting, not voting or social choice theory more broadly. In practice, this means that the survey begins with the work of Black and Farquharson and encompasses only the literature that builds pretty directly on their work.[1]

---

[1] A related line of research has recently emerged that is concerned with modelling rather specific institutional features of legislatures – and of the U.S. Congress in particular – such as bicameralism, committee and subcommittee structures, amendment control rules, etc. Often this literature takes account of the environment of incomplete information within which legislators typically operate. This essay does not attempt to encompass this developing literature; in particular, we do not deal with complex institutional arrangements and, in taking

1.1. Overview

The basic framework for the theory of voting is as follows. We have a (finite or infinite) set X of *alternatives*, which are the ultimate objects of choice, and a finite set N of *voters* endowed with *preferences* over alternatives. An *agenda*, i.e., a finite subset A of X, is formed and some *voting procedure* is employed. This generates, a *voting game*, in which each voter, on the basis of his preferences and certain behavioral assumptions, selects a *voting strategy*. The resulting collection of strategies determines the *voting outcome*.

The simplest voting problem arises when there are just two alternatives — call them x and y — on the agenda. In this case, voting by simple *majority rule* strikes most people as fair and reasonable. Each voter votes for x, or votes for y, or abstains, and whichever alternative receives more votes becomes the outcome. While there is the problem of ties, voting to choose between two alternatives is essentially straightforward.

More vexing problems arise when the agenda is expanded to three or more alternatives. It is fundamental that no democratic method of voting or social choice can then avoid problems of consistency and strategy. Commonly used voting procedures are of three broad types. An *aggregation* procedure asks voters to express some kind of preferences over the whole agenda and then tabulates ballots in a single step to determine the voting outcome. An *elimination* procedure initially tabulates ballots in some fashion, on the basis of which weaker alternatives are eliminated; ballots are then retabulated (or a runoff election is held) on the reduced set of alternatives; elimination and retabulation continue until every alternative but one has been eliminated. Aggregation and elimination procedures are commonly used in mass elections with multiple candidates, in which voters cannot assemble and cast repeated ballots.

In small voting bodies such as committees, legislatures, public meetings, etc., it is feasible and essentially invariable practice to use *sequential binary procedure* of the parliamentary type. A sequence of binary (e.g., yes/no) choices is put to the voters, the nature of later choices depending on the results of earlier votes. Each ballot, being binary, can be tabulated on the basis of majority rule; individual ballots thus avoid the problems of consistency and strategy that characterize voting more generally. The complexity arises in

---

account of strategic behavior by voters, we assume that they are operating in a context of complete information, in the manner of classical game theory.

structuring the sequence of votes that ultimately leads to the voting outcome and, in this larger structure, problems of consistency and strategy reappear.

Describing the general character of the voting problem, and of committee voting in particular, raises a variety of more specific questions.

Normative Questions   Given the preferences of the members of the voting group, which alternative ought to be selected as the voting outcome? And how ought the voting to be conducted?

Descriptive Questions   Given the preferences of the members of the voting group, which alternative will actually be selected as the voting outcome? What factors, in addition to the preferences of the group members, may affect the outcome?

Procedural Questions   What different procedures may the group use to narrow the initial set of alternatives down to an ultimate outcome? How may these procedures be formally described? And how does the choice of procedures affect the outcome?

Voting Order Questions   Three or more alternatives must be considered in some sequential fashion. Is the final outcome affected by the order in which alternatives are considered? And if so, is an alternative favored by coming earlier in the voting order or later?

Parliamentary Questions   In a parliamentary context, the set of alternatives is generated by proposed motions, amendments, substitute motions, substitute amendments, and so forth. How is the voting outcome affected by the parliamentary status of each alternative?

Strategic Questions   As votes are taken, members of the voting group must decide how to vote. Is it always is expedient for voters to vote according to their 'honest' or 'sincere' preferences or do they sometimes have an incentive to vote 'strategically'? If such strategic incentives exist, do they arise infrequently, commonly, or ubiquitously?

Equilibrium Questions   If voting is treated as a game of strategy by all members of the voting group, is it possible to identify 'best' voting strategies for all voters? If so, and if all voters use their best strategies, is the voting outcome different from what it would be if they all used 'honest' voting strategies? And if the outcomes are different, how do 'strategic' and 'honest' outcomes compare?

Coalition Formation Questions When is it expedient for voters to enter into coalitions and make explicit agreements as to how they will vote? And if all voters can form coalitions freely, is the voting outcome different from what it would otherwise be? And if the outcomes are different, how do 'cooperative' and 'noncooperative' outcomes compare?

Agenda Control Questions If one committee member can unilaterally control which alternatives, other than an implicit 'status quo' alternative, are placed on the agenda of alternatives, or the order in which alternatives are voted on or their parliamentary status, how much 'agenda control' can this member exercise? Under what conditions can voting outcomes be manipulated by expanding the agenda?

Agenda Formation Questions If one, or two, or several, or all committee members have the power to propose alternatives for consideration, what strategic considerations may affect their choices. Do such members have 'best' agenda-setting strategies? Does an agenda-setting 'equilibrium' result?

The literature on committee voting has now developed to a point that definite answers may be given to most of these questions. Sketching out the content of the remainder of this essay also sketches out the nature of the answers. In the remaining part of Section 1, we provide a description and analysis of choice between two alternatives in terms of 'vote counting rules,' of which simple majority rule is by far the most prominent example. In Section 2, we use the language of sets and trees to describe, categorize, and analyze voting agendas generated by procedures of the sequential binary type, and we examine the linkage between the parliamentary language of motions, amendments, substitutes, etc., and such agendas. In Section 3, we describe voter preferences and identify plausible restrictions on these preferences that model different contexts of political choice. We also examine collective — and particularly majority — preferences of the whole set of voters. In Section 4, we define 'honest' or 'sincere' voting behavior, and we see that it is often not expedient to vote in such a fashion. We also provide a definition of 'strategic' or 'sophisticated' voting behavior and show that, given any sequential binary procedure, a 'voting game' ordinarily entails a determinate voting outcome. Finally, we define 'cooperative' voting behavior, allowing for the free formation of voting coalitions. In Section 5, we examine the existence and nature of 'best' alternatives in terms of collective preferences. This discussion is relevant to the normative question of which alternative ought to be selected and provides concepts for subsequent descriptive analysis. In Section 6, we present algorithms for determining voting outcomes under certain standard procedures. We examine the effects of agenda structures, voting order, and the parliamentary status of alternatives, on outcomes. We find that these effects depend very much on whether voting behavior is sincere, sophisticated, or cooperative, and we compare outcomes under these different behavioral assumptions. In Section 7, we examine the question of agenda control and particularly note how the efficacy of agenda control is importantly dependent on whether the subsequent behavior of voters is sincere or sophisticated. In Section 8, we consider various processes of agenda formation and the strategic problems faced by agenda setters according to the degree of competition they face.

1.2. Vote Counting Rules

We have observed that voting to choose between two alternatives is essentially straightforward. The kind of sequential binary voting procedure characteristically used by committees and parliamentary bodies subdivides a voting problem into a sequence of binary choices. In the next section, we consider how this sequencing may be structured. Here we consider how binary choices may be made at each step in the sequence.[2]

There is set $N = 1, \ldots, n$ of *eligible voters* (where the number of voters $|N| = n$) who must choose between two options: m (e.g., acceptance of a motion) and *not m* (e.g., rejection of a motion), which we designate ϕ. Each voter i must cast a vote V_i in one of three ways:

$$V_i = +1, \quad \text{representing a vote for } m;$$
$$V_i = 0, \quad \text{representing abstention; and}$$
$$V_i = -1, \quad \text{representing a vote for } \phi.$$

A (binary) *vote counting rule* F gives, for every *configuration* (or 'roll call') $V = (V_1, \ldots, V_n)$ of votes, one of three *results*:

---

[2]The following is adapted, very broadly, from May (1952) and Fishburn (1973: Part I). Terminology pertaining to properties of vote counting rules borrows more generally from social choice theory. Note that a vote counting rule, as defined here and as commonly employed in a parliamentary setting, is deterministic and entails no random element.

$F(V) = +1,$ representing selection of m;
$F(V) = 0,$ representing a tie between m and ϕ; and
$F(V) = -1,$ representing selection of ϕ.

Let $n(+1)$, $n(0)$, and $n(-1)$ be the number of voters who cast each type of vote, and let n' be the number of *non-abstaining* voters, i.e., $n' = n(+1) + n(-1)$.

Now we can define several common vote counting rules. The most common is (simple) *relative majority* (or *plurality*) *rule*, according to which:

$$F(V) = +1 \quad \text{if and only if } n(+1) > n'/2;$$
$$F(V) = -1 \quad \text{if and only if } n(+1) < n'/2; \text{ and}$$
$$F(V) = 0 \quad \text{if and only if } n(+1) = n'/2.$$

Another is (simple) *absolute majority rule*, according to which:

$$F(V) = +1 \quad \text{if and only if } n(+1) > n/2;$$
$$F(V) = -1 \quad \text{if and only if } n(-1) > n/2; \text{ and}$$
$$F(V) = 0 \quad \text{otherwise.}$$

In the event voters never abstain, the two variants of majority rule are equivalent.

A more general class of vote counting rules is 'supra-majority rule,' each variant of which is given by a *decision rule d* such that $0.5 < d \leq 1$. According to *relative* (or *absolute*) *supra-majority rule*:

$$F(V) = +1 \quad \text{if and only if } n(+1) \geq d \times n'(\text{or } d \times n);$$
$$F(V) = -1 \quad \text{if and only if } n(-1) \geq d \times n'(\text{or } d \times n); \text{ and}$$
$$F(V) = 0 \quad \text{otherwise.}$$

If $d = 1$, we have *unanimity rule*; as d approaches its lower limit of 0.5, we get simple majority rule. In the U.S., $d = 2/3$ is rather commonly used (e.g., on treaties, constitutional amendments, veto overrides, etc.).

We now consider some conditions that may apply to vote counting rules. A vote counting rule is *anonymous* if $F(V') = F(V)$ whenever V' is merely a rearrangement of the elements of V. That is, $F(V')$ and $F(V)$ always give the same result if V' and V have the same *number* of $+1$s, 0s, and -1s, respectively, even though they may be cast by different voters. Every variant of majority rule is anonymous.

A vote counting rule is *responsive to voter i* if there are two vote configurations V and V' such that (i) $V_i' \neq V_i$, (ii) $V_j' = V_j$ for all j other than i, and (iii) $F(V') \neq F(V)$. In words, a vote counting rule is responsive to voter i if there is some configuration of other votes in which i's vote 'makes a difference.' A vote counting rule is *fully responsive* if it is responsive to every eligible voter. Every variant of majority rule is fully responsive.

A voting counting rule is *non-negatively responsive* if, for every pair of vote configurations V and V' such that $V_i' \geq V_i$ (or $V_i' \leq V_i$) for every voter i, it follows that $F(V') \geq F(V)$ (or $F(V') \leq F(V)$, respectively) — that is, in so far as the vote counting rule is responsive, it responds in the 'right' way. Every variant of majority rule is non-negatively responsive.

A vote counting rule is *neutral* if $F(V_1, \ldots, V_n) = -F(-V_1, \ldots, -V_n)$. Put otherwise, a neutral vote counting rule treats the two options m and ϕ symmetrically. Every variant of majority rule (as defined above) is neutral.

A vote counting rule F' is *more resolute* than another rule F if $F'(V) = 0$ implies $F(V) = 0$ but not conversely. If $d < d'$, d-majority rule is more resolute than d'-majority rule, given a sufficently large number n votes. Likewise the relative version of any rule is more resolute than the absolute version of the same rule.

A vote counting rule F is *almost resolute* if it is true that if (i) $F(V) = 0$, (ii) $V_i' \neq V_i$ for any voter i, and (iii) $V_j' = V_j$ for all voters j other i, then $F(V) \neq 0$. This says that the tie result is a 'knife-edge' condition, in that a tie is broken if any voter changes his vote in any way. Simple relative majority rule is almost resolute and is the only variant of majority rule to be so.

A vote counting rule is *positively responsive* if it is both non-negatively responsive and almost resolute. *May's (1952) Majority Rule Theorem* says this: *a vote counting rule is anonymous, neutral, and positively responsive if and only if it is simple relative majority rule.* Henceforth, any unqualified reference to 'majority rule' should be understood as referring to simple relative majority rule.

A vote counting rule is *resolute* if it is never true that $F(V) = 0$. Simple majority rule is resolute in the special case in which (i) no voter abstains *and* (ii) the number n of voters is odd. But, in general, a resolute vote counting rule must violate either anonymity or neutrality. Simple majority rule can be made resolute rule in either of two ways. Anonymity can be (slightly) violated, so that there is a distinguished voter (e.g., a 'chairman') whose vote breaks any tie. (Even this assures resoluteness only if the 'chairman' never abstains.) Or neutrality can be (slightly) violated so that a tie is broken in favor the favored option. The latter is the tie-breaking device most commonly used in parliamentary bodies, with ϕ (rejection of the motion) being the favored alternative. Thus any variant of majority rule can be rendered resolute as follows:

$$F(V) = +1 \quad \text{if and only if } n(+1) \geq d \times n'(\text{or } d \times n); \text{ and}$$
$$F(V) = -1 \quad \text{otherwise.}$$

The *standard parliamentary vote counting rule* is the resolute variant of simple relative majority rule.

2. VOTING AGENDAS

Under sequential binary procedure of the sort used by committees, a voting *agenda* specifies the 'motions' or 'questions' that are put to a vote and the order in which these votes occur. This is equivalent to saying that the agenda specifies the alternatives that are possible voting outcomes and the particular sequence of votes by which this set is winnowed down to a final outcome.

2.1. Agendas, Alternatives, and Proposals

The *agenda set A* is a finite subset of alternatives that are put before the committee for voting. Often it is natural to use the word 'agenda' to refer simply to this set of alternatives (as was done in the introductory section). But in its more precise sense, the agenda also specifies the *particular sequence of 'questions'* put before the committee for voting, according to which it will arrive at the final outcome. The nature of this sequence of votes, or *agenda structure*, depends in turn on two further matters: the character of the *voting procedure* in use and the *voting order* in which questions are brought up for consideration under this procedure.

The agenda set *A* is generated by *proposals* made by committee members. These proposals may be designated 'motions,' 'bills,' 'amendments,' 'substitutes,' etc., according to the order in which they are proposed and relevant parliamentary usage. These designations influence the structure of the agenda and, in particular, the order in which alternatives are voted on.

It is crucial to recognize that the set of *alternatives* and the set of *proposals* generally do not coincide. Almost always the set of alternatives is larger than the set of proposals. First, virtually always a committee has available the alternative of 'doing nothing,' which inaction has the effect of maintaining the *status quo* or effecting a reversion to some pre-established alternative (e.g., some level of taxation and/or expenditure). This alternative is always available to the committee as a possible outcome, though typically it is not explicitly proposed. We refer to this distinguished element of A as the *status quo alternative*, which in this section we designate ϕ. Thus, even if just one motion m is proposed, a committee faces a choice, i.e., whether to accept or reject this motion, and two alternatives are on the agenda: (1) to accept the motion (m) and to reject the motion and maintain the status quo (ϕ).

The set of alternatives further exceeds the set of proposals whenever two or more *compatible* proposals are offered — that is, proposals that are literally not *alternatives* to one another, because they are not mutually exclusive. Suppose two compatible bills or amendments to a bill are proposed. These two proposals generate four alternatives: (1) adoption of both, (2) adoption of the first and rejection of the second, (3) rejection of the first and adoption of the second, and (4) rejection of both.

Under parliamentary voting of the sequential binary type, the *number of votes taken* is typically equal to the *number of proposals made*, as each proposal generates a 'question' and there is a vote on each question. The number of votes thus typically falls short of the number of alternatives.

Each sequential binary vote is typically a yes/no vote on the question of accepting some proposal, for example: 'Is the substitute amendment accepted?', 'Is the amendment to the motion accepted?', 'Is the bill as amended adopted?' These yes/no votes implicitly entail paired comparisons between alternatives or sets of alternatives. To demonstrate this and to fix intuitively the notion of a voting agenda, let us consider a variety of examples.

2.2. Agenda Examples

Agenda Example 1   Consider the simplest non-trivial case of parliamentary voting: a motion m is introduced and a single amendment a is proposed. These two proposals generate an agenda set of three alternatives, as follows:

m :   adoption of the motion (unamended);
$m + a$:   adoption of the motion perfected by the amendment; and
ϕ :   rejection of the motion.

In Anglo-American legislatures, yes/no votes would be taken in turn on these questions.

> *Question 1.*   Is the amendment accepted?
> *Question 2.*   Is the motion (as amended or not) accepted?

If the amendment is accepted, the committee then chooses between $m + a$ and ϕ; if the amendment is rejected, the committee then chooses between m and ϕ. In either event, ϕ remains as a possible outcome after the first vote. Thus, at the first vote, the committee is effectively choosing between m and $m + a$, and the agenda may be summarized by the following implicit pairings of alternatives, where each number refers to a vote:

> 1. $m + a$ vs. m;
> 2. winner of 1 vs. ϕ.

Agenda Example 2   We might regard the labelling of the alternatives as m, $m + a$, and ϕ to be somewhat arbitrary. For example, amendment a may add some language to motion m; but it could just as well be that the original motion includes the language and an amendment is offered to strike it. Labelling the status quo alternative is less arbitrary, yet in the long run the nature of the prevailing status quo depends on previous acts of the committee or on external events. Thus Agenda Example 1 (with the three alternatives generically labelled x, y, and z) has three variants according to which alternative has which parliamentary status (original motion, motion as amended, status quo) and, as a result, according to the *order* in which proposals are made and alternatives are voted on.

> *Agenda Example 2a.*
> 1. x vs. y;
> 2. winner of 1 vs. z

> *Agenda Example 2b.*
> 1. x vs. z;
> 2. winner of 1 vs. y

> *Agenda Example 2c.*
> 1. y vs. z;
> 2. winner of 1 vs. x

Agenda Example 3   To complicate matters a bit, suppose that a motion m is proposed, then an amendment a to the motion, and finally an amendment a' to the amendment. (Proposal a' is a *second-order* amendment, as it pertains to the previous amendment, not to the original motion.) These three proposals generate an agenda set of four alternatives, as follows:

m :	adoption of the motion (unamended);
$m + a$:	adoption of the motion perfected by the (unamended) amendment;
$m + a'$:	adoption of the motion perfected by the amended amendment; and
ϕ :	rejection of the motion.

In Anglo-American legislatures, voting would take place as follows.

Question 1.	Is the amendment to the amendment accepted?
Question 2.	Is the amendment (as amended or not) accepted?
Question 3.	Is the motion (as amended or not) accepted?

As before, the agenda may be summarized by the following implicit pairings:

1. $m + a'$ vs. $m + a$;
2. winner of 1 vs. m;
3. winner of 2 vs. ϕ.

Agenda Example 4   Generalizing from these examples suggests the following stylized structure for any agenda set A with generically labelled alternatives $x_0, x_1, \ldots, x_m$, where the subscripts indicate the *order of voting*:

1. x_0 vs. x_1;
2. winner of 1 vs. x_2;
......
k. winner of $k - 1$ vs. x_k;
......
m. winner of $m - 1$ vs. x_m.[3]

Black (1948) (1958) originally considered such a generalized sequential binary procedure, calling it *ordinary committee procedure*. Farquharson

---

[3]We begin with the subscript 0 because, when we consider the parliamentary status of alternatives (as in Agenda Examples 4a and 4b), it is convenient to designate the status quo x_0.

(1969a) showed that voting on amendments of successively higher orders resulted in an agenda of this type, which he accordingly called *amendment procedure*. Given an agenda with k alternatives, amendment procedure generates $k!/2$ distinct agenda variants, each entailing $k-1$ votes, according to the order in which the k alternatives are voted on.

Agenda Example 4a If we take account of the parliamentary status of alternatives, we shall adopt the convention that the subscripts designate the order in which alternatives were generated by proposals, so x_0 is the status quo, x_1 is the initial motion, x_2 is the motion with the initial amendment, and so forth. Under standard Anglo-American parliamentary procedure (exemplified by Agenda Examples 1 and 3), amendment agendas are — to use the terminology of Shepsle and Weingast (1984) — *backwards-built*, in that the voting order is the *reverse* of the order in which alternatives were generated and accordingly the reverse of the order of the subscripts. We call such an agenda — particularly one that put the status quo last in the voting order — a *standard amendment agenda*. The generic standard amendment agenda is therefore:

1. x_m vs. x_{m-1};
2. winner of 1 vs. x_{m-2};
......
k. winner of $k-1$ vs. x_{m-k};
......
m. winner of $m-1$ vs. x_0.

More generally, we call any agenda in which some alternative is invariably paired with the status quo at the final vote a *standard agenda*.

Agenda Example 4b In less formal settings, amendment agendas may be *forward-built* — that is, the voting order is the same as the order which alternatives were generated. Voting would take place as follows:

Question 1.   Shall the status quo be replaced by the first proposed alternative?

Question 2.   Shall the (perhaps revised) status quo (i.e. the winner of the first vote) be replaced by the second proposed alternative?

Question 3.   And so forth.[4]

---

[4] Such an agenda resembles what Wilson (1986) calls a *forward-moving agenda*, except that in the latter each vote is taken before the next proposal is made.

The resulting agenda is just that shown for Agenda Example 4, if we now specify that the alternatives are subscripted to reflect the order in which they were generated. Note that Agenda Examples 4a and 4b have identical *structures* but opposite *voting orders*.

Many results in the theory of voting pertain specifically to amendment agendas. But, taking note of an influential article by Ordeshook and Schwartz (1987) which points out that much actual parliamentary voting does not take place under such agendas, we should also consider agendas that do not fit the amendment pattern.

Agenda Example 5 Suppose that a bill b is introduced, an amendment a to the bill is proposed, then a substitute bill s, and finally an amendment a' to the substitute bill. These are the alternatives:

b : passage of the original bill (unamended);
$b + a$: passage of the original bill perfected by its amendment;
s : passage of the substitute bill (unamended);
$s + a'$: passage of the substitute bill perfected by its amendment; and
ϕ : rejection of any bill.

In the U.S. Congress and most Anglo-American legislatures, voting would proceed as follows.

Question 1. Is the amendment to the original bill accepted?
Question 2. Is the amendment to the substitute bill accepted?
Question 3. Is the substitute bill (as amended or not) accepted (in place of the original bill, as amended or not)?
Question 4 . Is the surviving bill (original or substitute, as amended or not) accepted?

The agenda implicitly pairs alternatives in this fashion:

1. b vs. $b + a$;
2. s vs. $s + a'$;
3. winner of 1 vs. winner of 2;
4. winner of 3 vs. ϕ.

This agenda departs from the standard amendment pattern by being *discontinuous*, in that the winner at vote 1 does not enter the following vote but is set aside for later consideration (at vote 3). This is an example of what Banks (1989) calls *two-stage amendment procedure*, under which an original bill is perfected under amendment procedure, a substitute bill perfected under amendment procedure, a choice is made between the two perfected bills, and finally a choice is made between the surviving bill and the status quo. (There might be additional amendments pertaining to the original and substitute bills. Also a substitute amendment might be proposed, generating a *three-stage amendment agenda* or one two-stage agenda nested within another.)

Agenda Example 6 Suppose a motion m is introduced, an amendment a_1 is moved, and then another amendment a_2 is moved that is *compatible* with the first — that is, both are *first-order* amendments in that they both pertain to the original motion, they are not mutually exclusive, and both may be incorporated into the surviving bill. The alternatives are as follows:

$$
\begin{array}{rl}
m : & \text{adoption of the original motion (unamended);} \\
m + a_1 : & \text{adoption of the motion perfected by the first} \\
 & \text{amendment only;} \\
m + a_2 : & \text{adoption of the motion perfected by the second} \\
 & \text{amendment only;} \\
m + a_1 + a_2 : & \text{adoption of the motion perfected by both} \\
 & \text{amendments; and} \\
\phi : & \text{rejection of the motion.}
\end{array}
$$

These three proposals generate five alternatives, because the two amendments are compatible. (By the same token, a single amendment corresponding to $a_1 + a_2$ might be offered. Then, under standard parliamentary procedure, any committee member could request *division of the question* into its component parts, so that separate votes would be taken on a_1 and a_2.) In Congress and most Anglo-American legislatures, three votes would be taken.[5]

---

[5] Standard parliamentary procedure would require that this be what Ordeshook and Schwartz (1987) call a *multi-period agenda* — that is, amendment a_1 must be voted up or down before amendment a_2 is formally introduced. It may be reasonable to suppose, however, that it is generally known at the time a_1 is voted on that a_2 will be proposed. Note that a forward moving agenda is also multi-period. In any event, we assume that the whole voting agenda is known before any voting takes place.

Question 1.   Is the first amendment accepted?
Question 2.   Is the second amendment accepted?
Question 3.   Is the motion (as it may be amended) accepted?

In this case, it is not really true that two alternatives are paired at the first vote, but we might summarize the agenda as follows:

1. m vs. $m + a_1$;
2. $\begin{cases} m \text{ vs. } m + a_2, \text{ if } m \text{ wins at 1} \\ m + a_1 \text{ vs. } m + a_1 + a_2, \text{ if } m + a_1 \text{ wins at 1;} \end{cases}$;
3. winner of 2 vs. ϕ.

The way in which this agenda departs from an amendment agenda is indicated by the way in which the specification of *both* alternatives paired at the second vote is contingent upon the result of the first vote (though the agenda is *continuous* — in either contingency, the winner of the first vote enters the second vote). Directly related is the fact that this agenda is *incomplete* — that is, it is possible (in this case, certain) that some alternative never enters the voting (i.e., $m + a_2$ if $m + a_1$ wins the first vote, and $m + a_1 + a_2$ if m wins the first vote). For this reason, the number of votes falls *two* short of the number of alternatives. Precisely because this agenda is incomplete, the informal specification of the agenda in terms of pairwise votes is not entirely appropriate. We shall return to this point in the next subsection, where we present an analytical device that both identifies and sidesteps this ambiguity.

Agenda Example 7   Incompleteness arises more profoundly if we consider a type of agenda commonly used in informal voting bodies, which was employed in Plott and Levine's (1976) pioneering experimental study of agenda influence on voting outcomes. To use their introductory example, suppose that a group must decide what kind of banquet to give and that two questions have been raised.

Question 1 :   Shall the dress be formal or informal?
Question 2 :   Shall the cuisine be French or Mexican?

These two questions generate four alternatives:

x :   formal dress, French cuisine;
y :   informal dress, French cuisine;
z :   formal dress, Mexican cuisine; and
v :   informal dress, Mexican cuisine.

Each question, though not yes/no, is binary, and a sequential binary agenda results. Given two questions, the agenda has two variants, according to which question is put to a vote first. In general, the raising of k dichotomous questions generates $k!$ variants of an incomplete agenda with 2^k alternatives but only k votes.

What Ferejohn (1975; also see Kramer, 1972) calls a *bill-by-bill* agenda can arise in a formal parliamentary setting and is structurally equivalent to an agenda of the Plott–Levine type. Consider a set of bills, each of which may be independently passed or defeated. An alternative is complete specification of bills defeated and passed.[6] (Alternatively, an 'omnibus' bill corresponding to a particular alternative might be proposed at the outset, followed by a request for division of the question.) As illustrated by the dress/cuisine example, such agendas can be specified by listing the 'questions' in order but, because they are profoundly incomplete, they cannot be specified by listing pairwise votes between alternatives.

A generalization of a bill-by-bill agenda is what is commonly called *issue-by-issue* voting, in which each bill (or issue) may have a multiplicity (potentially even an infinite number) of positions. A position is chosen (perhaps under amendment procedure) on the first issue, then on the second, and so forth.

Agenda Example 8 All agendas we have considered thus far are *uniform*, in that the same number of votes is taken regardless of the results of earlier votes. But agendas need not be uniform. The most prominent example results from what Farquharson (1966 and 1969a) calls *successive procedure*. For example, suppose a motion m, an amendment a, and a second-order amendment a' are proposed, as in Agenda Example 3. Instead of following amendment procedure, the first vote might be on the 'question of principle' of whether to change the status quo; if this question fails, no further votes are taken. Only if the question of principle is decided favorably are more specific amendment considered. Thus the committee might vote on these questions.

Question 1 : Should the status quo ϕ be modified?
Question 2 : If so, should the original motion m be amended?

---

[6]This is certainly a multi-period agenda. Note that compatible first-order amendments (as in Agenda Example 6) generate an 'amendment-by-amendment' agenda 'standardized' by a final vote against the status quo.

Question 3 :   If so, should the original amendment *a* be
                  modified by the second-order amendment *a'*?

Agenda Example 9   Alternatively, the committee might vote on these
questions.

Question 1 :   Should the amended motion modified by the
                  second-order amendment *a'* be accepted?
Question 2 :   If not, should the amended motion *a* be adopted?
Question 3 :   If not, should the original motion *m* be accepted?

We call this a *sequential* agenda, though the term 'successive' is often applied
to this kind of agenda as well. This is because Agenda Examples 8 and 9 are
structurally equivalent; in both, alternatives are voted up or down in a fixed
order, and voting terminates once an alternative is voted up. The difference
is that, in Agenda Example 8, the voting order follows the order in which
alternatives were generated by proposals, while in Agenda Example 9, the
voting order is the reverse of this. Put otherwise, Agenda Example 8 is
forward-built, while Agenda Example 9 is backward-built.[7] Agendas of the
latter type are commonly used in continental European legislatures (Bjurulf
and Niemi, 1982; Rasch, 1987).

2.3. Agenda Structures

It is useful to have some general method for representing the structure of
sequential binary voting agendas. Farquharson (1956a, 1969a) devised a
convenient tool for describing a wide class of voting procedures, including
all those of the sequential binary type, which we call the *agenda tree*.[8]

---

[7]Ordeshook and Schwartz (1987: p. 182) observe that agendas similar to Agenda Example
9 may occur even in an Anglo-American legislature, when it is 'obliged to take some action (to
adopt a budget, say) and so must keep voting on proposed actions until one passes.' Farquharson
(1966) first introduced the term 'successive procedure,' which he interpreted in the manner of
Agenda Example 8. In his book (1969a) and in much voting theory, the voting order is taken
as given and is not related to the parliamentary status of alternatives, so the distinction between
Agenda Examples 8 and 9 disappears; the term 'successive,' may then be employed to cover
the agenda structure common to both.

[8]The following generally follows the formalization presented by McKelvey and Niemi
(1978); similar but less formal descriptions are given in Miller (1977b), McKelvey (1981),
Dummett (1984: Chapter 3), and elsewhere, as well as by Farquharson. Much of the
terminology is adapted from Ordeshook and Schwartz (1987), but their method of representing
an agenda structure differs from the more standard one presented here (see footnote 11).

A sequential binary voting process has a number of possible *outcomes*, each corresponding to selection of a particular alternative from the agenda. At the outset, the whole agenda set A constitutes the set of possible outcomes. As a result of a sequence of binary votes, alternatives are eliminated as possible outcomes, until but one remains — the actual voting outcome. The agenda tree graphically depicts all possible ways in which the initial set of alternatives may be narrowed down to a single outcome.

Intuitively, a 'tree' is a branching structure, with a single starting point and many end points. More formally a tree is a type of *directed graph*, i.e., a finite set V of *nodes* together with *directed lines* (arrows) between certain *ordered pairs* of nodes. A directed graph is *asymmetric* if, for any pair of nodes v and v', an arrow from v to v' precludes an arrow from v' to v. A directed graph is *complete* if, for any pair of nodes v and v', there is an arrow from v to v' or from v' to v; otherwise it is *incomplete*. A *path* from node v to node v' is a sequence of two or more distinct nodes, beginning with v and ending with v' such that there is an arrow from each node to the following node; v' is *reachable* from v if there is a path from v to v'. A *tree* is an asymmetric directed graph such that: (1) there is a unique *initial node* with no incoming arrows; and (2) there is at most one path from one node to another. It follows that there is exactly one path from the initial node to each other node. The *order* of node v is the number of steps in this path. If there is an arrow from v to v', we say v' *follows* v and call the arrow a *branch*.

The following points derive straightforwardly (Harary, Norman and Cartwright, 1965: pp. 283–286). In a tree: (1) every other node is reachable from the initial node and this is true of no other node; (2) every node, other than the initial node, follows exactly one other node; and (3) there is a nonempty subset of nodes, called *terminal nodes*, from which no other node is reachable.

A *binary tree* is a tree such that exactly *two* nodes follow each non-terminal node. In a binary tree, the two nodes following a non-terminal node v can be denoted v_0 (following via the 'left-hand' branch) and v_1 (following via the 'right-hand' branch).

A *binary agenda tree* is defined by an agenda set A of alternatives, a binary tree with at least as many terminal nodes as there are alternatives in A, and a function Γ which assigns a one-element subset of A to each terminal node so that (i) every one-element subset of A is assigned to at least one terminal node and (ii), for every pair of terminal nodes v_0 and v_1 following the same node v, $\Gamma(v_0)$ and $\Gamma(v_1)$ are distinct.

In an agenda tree, each non-terminal node represents the occasion for a vote and is called a *decision node*. Each terminal node represents the final outcome of a particular sequence of votes and is called an *outcome node*. A decision node such that *both* following nodes are outcome nodes is called a *final* decision node.

Consider Agenda Example 1, the agenda tree for which is depicted in Figure 1. The initial node v represents the first vote (on the question accepting the amendment). The two nodes of order 1 represent the second vote on the question of adopting the motion, in the event the amendment fails (v_0) or succeeds (v_1). (Throughout, we follow the convention that the left-hand branch of an agenda tree is followed in the event the question put to a vote fails and the right-hand branch is followed in the event the question succeeds.) The four terminal nodes represent the ends of the four distinct *voting paths* and each entails a particular outcome. Following the indexing convention just noted, the assignment function Γ is as follows:

$$\Gamma(v_{00}) = \{\phi\}; \qquad \Gamma(v_{10}) = \{\phi\}; \quad \text{and}$$
$$\Gamma(v_{01}) = \{m\}; \qquad \Gamma(v_{11}) = \{m + a\}.$$

Note that two votes are taken in any case, so all paths from the initial node to a terminal node are of the same length. Though there are only three alternatives, the tree has four outcome nodes. This occurs because the outcome $\{\phi\}$ can be reached by two distinct paths: rejection of the amendment followed by rejection of the motion, and acceptance of the amendment followed by rejection of the motion. Figures 2–8 show agenda trees for other Agenda Examples. (While in Figure 1 the nodes are labelled generically, in Figures 2–8 nodes are labelled by their 'reachable sets,' as defined just below.)

Associated with each node v of an agenda tree over A is some subset $\Gamma(v)$ of *outcomes reachable from* v. At any outcome node v, $\Gamma(v)$ is the one-element set given by the assignment function Γ discussed above. At any decision node v, $\Gamma(v)$ is a multi-element set defined as follows: an alternative x belongs to $\Gamma(v)$ if and only if there is some outcome node v' such that v' is reachable from v and $\Gamma(v') = \{x\}$. Two consequences follow immediately from this definition: (1) for the initial node v^*, $\Gamma(v^*) = A$; and (2) at for any pair of nodes v_0 and v_1 following node v, the union of $\Gamma(v_0)$ and $\Gamma(v_1)$ coincides with $\Gamma(v)$. For the decision nodes in Figure 1,

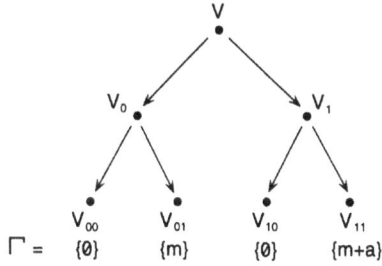

FIGURE 1 An Amendment Agenda Tree with a Single Amendment (Agenda Example 1)

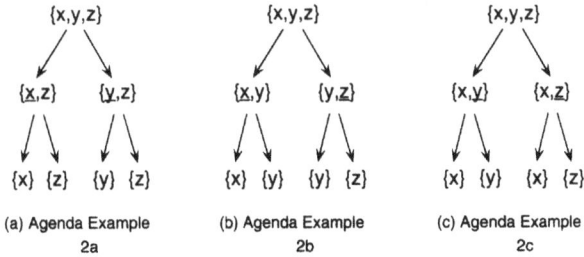

FIGURE 2 Amendment Agenda Tree Variants with Three Alternatives (Agenda Example 2)

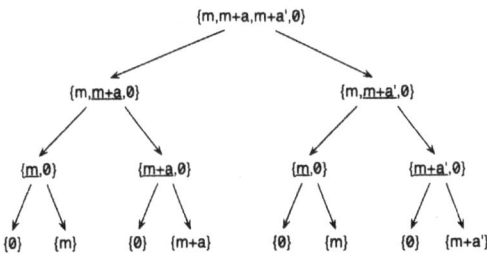

FIGURE 3 An Amendment Agenda Tree with a Second-order Amendment (Agenda Example 3)

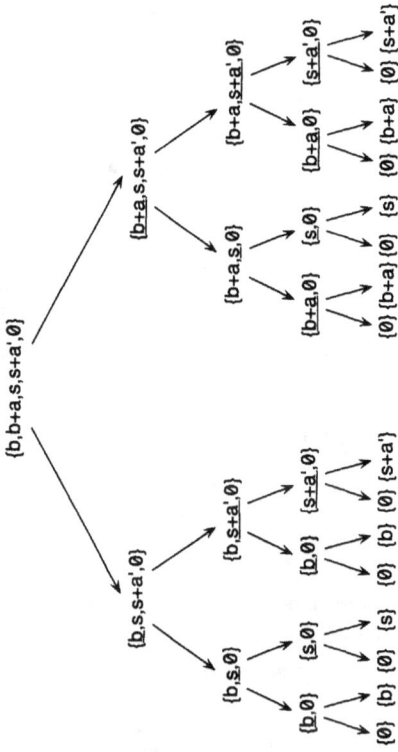

FIGURE 4   An Agenda Tree with a Substitute Bill (Agenda Example 5)

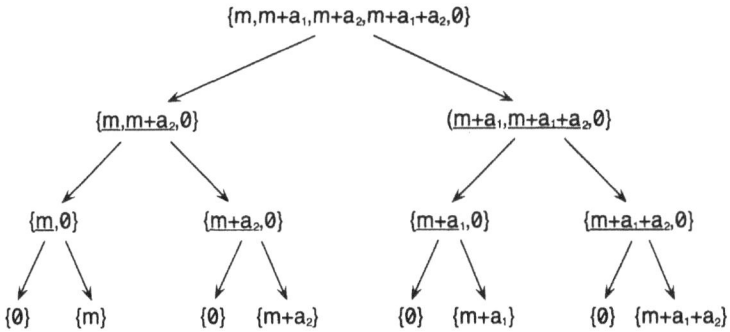

FIGURE 5 An Agenda Tree with Two First-order Amendments (Agenda Example 6)

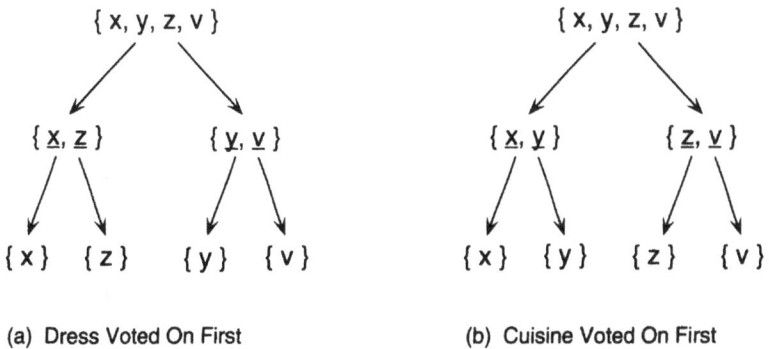

(a) Dress Voted On First   (b) Cuisine Voted On First

FIGURE 6 Uniform Partition (Plott-Levine/Bill-by-Bill) Agenda Tree Variants (Agenda Example 7)

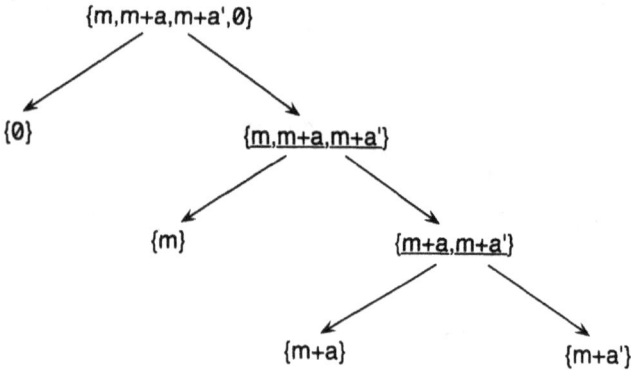

FIGURE 7 A Successive Agenda Tree (Agenda Example 8)

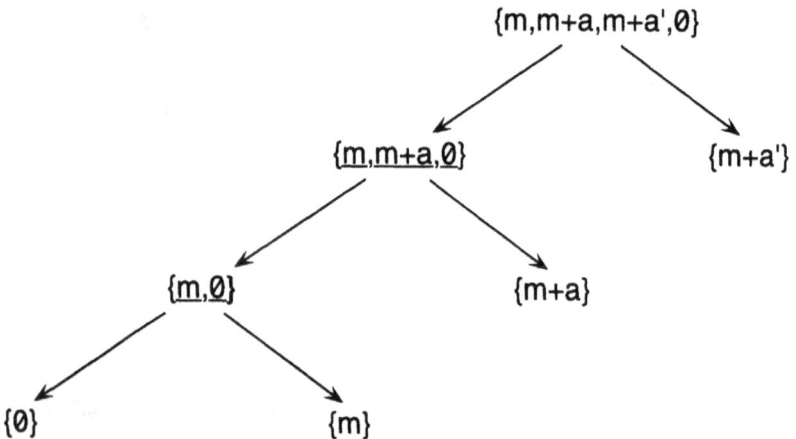

FIGURE 8 A Sequential Agenda Tree (Agenda Example 9)

these *reachable sets* are: $\Gamma(v) = \{m, m + a, \phi\}$, $\Gamma(v_0) = \{m, \phi\}$, and $\Gamma(v_1) = \{m + a, \phi\}$. Reachable sets identify nodes in Figures 2–8 and subsequent agenda diagrams.

Consequence (2) above implies that each of $\Gamma(v_0)$ and $\Gamma(v_1)$ is a subset of $\Gamma(v)$. Here (and following Farquharson, 1969a, p. 11) we make the additional assumption that each is a *proper* subset. Substantively, this means we restrict our attention to *non-repetitive* agendas, i.e., those under which the effect of every vote is to eliminate *at least one* alternative as a possible outcome.[9]

For any decision node v, let $\Gamma^*(v)$ be the intersection of $\Gamma(v_0)$ and $\Gamma(v_1)$. Substantively, $\Gamma^*(v)$ is the set of possible outcomes before vote v is taken that will remain as possible outcomes after vote v is taken, *regardless of the result of the vote*. We may thus characterize $\Gamma^*(v)$ as the set of alternatives that are *unchallenged* at v. All alternatives in $\Gamma(v)$ and not in $\Gamma^*(v)$ are *challenged* at v. The set of alternatives challenged at v is partitioned into two disjoint *surviving* sets $\Gamma'(v_0)$ and $\Gamma'(v_1)$ at the following nodes. Put otherwise, $\Gamma'(v_0)$ is the subset of alternatives in $\Gamma(v_0)$ that do not also belong to $\Gamma(v_1)$, and likewise for $\Gamma'(v_1)$. ($\Gamma'(v)$ is not defined at the initial node v.) Substantively, $\Gamma'(v_0)$ is the set of alternatives that were challenged at vote v but still survive as possible outcomes at v_0, and likewise for $\Gamma'(v_1)$. For the non-initial decision nodes in Figure 1, the surviving sets are $\Gamma'(v_0) = \{m\}$ and $\Gamma'(v_1) = \{m + a\}$. Figures 2–8 show the sets $\Gamma'(v)$ at each non-initial decision node v by underlining the elements of $\Gamma(v)$ that belong to $\Gamma'(v)$.

Now we can more formally define various properties of sequential binary agendas. An agenda is *uniform* if all of its outcome nodes are of the same order; otherwise, an agenda is *non-uniform*. Substantively, under a uniform agenda a fixed number of votes is taken, whereas under a non-uniform agenda the result of an earlier vote may determine whether a later vote is taken. Of the agendas we have considered, only the successive and sequential types (Agenda Examples 8 and 9) are non-uniform.

An agenda is *complete* if, for any node v, the number of elements in its reachable set $\Gamma(v)$ is no less than $k - h$, where k is the size of the agenda set and h is he order of node v; otherwise, an agenda is *incomplete*. Substantively, under a complete agenda no more than one alternative can be eliminated as a possible outcome at any vote, whereas under an incomplete agenda two or more alternatives may be eliminated. In an agenda that is both complete and non-repetitive, the number of elements in $\Gamma(v)$ is precisely $k - h$; such an agenda is necessarily uniform, every outcome node being of order $k - 1$, and exactly one alternative is eliminated as a possible outcome at every vote. Among the agendas we have considered, amendment agendas (Agenda Examples 1–4) and their two-stage (or multi-stage) variants (Agenda Example 5) are complete, and the others are incomplete.

---

[9]This means we do not consider agendas that include preliminary votes (the results of which can be reversed by subsequent votes) or procedural votes.

An agenda is *continuous* if, at every decision node v, whenever x belongs to $\Gamma'(v)$, x also belongs to either $\Gamma'(v_0)$ or $\Gamma'(v_1)$; otherwise, an agenda is *discontinuous*. Substantively, under a continuous agenda any alternative that is once challenged continues to be challenged as long as it survives or until it becomes the voting outcome. Of the agendas we have considered, only two-stage (or multi-stage) amendment agendas (Agenda Example 5) are discontinuous.

An agenda is *symmetric* if the assignment function Γ works in a symmetric fashion in this sense: at every decision node v, (i) $|\Gamma(v_0)| = |\Gamma(v_1)|$ (where $|S|$ is the number of elements in the set S) and (ii) the subagenda beginning at v_0 is equivalent to the subagenda beginning at node v_1 if the elements of $\Gamma'(v_1)$ replace those of $\Gamma'(v_0)$ or *vice versa*. Put more substantively, under a symmetric agenda the result of a given vote determines only *what* alternatives survive as possible outcomes, not the *structure* of the remaining agenda. A symmetric agenda is necessarily uniform. All uniform agendas we have considered are symmetric. An example of a non-symmetric agenda is provided by what Banks (1989) calls a *two-stage conditional amendment agenda*. In such an agenda, the voting order on the substitute and its variants is conditioned on which variant of the original bill has survived.

A *partition agenda* is an agenda such that, at every decision node v, the sets $\Gamma(v_0)$ and $\Gamma(v_1)$ constitute a partition in $\Gamma(v)$. Given a partition agenda, $\Gamma^*(v)$ is empty and $\Gamma'(v) = \Gamma(v)$ for every non-initial node v. In words, every reachable alternative is challenged at every vote. Given more than two alternatives, partition agendas are necessarily incomplete. Successive (or sequential) and bill-by-bill (or Plott–Levine) agendas are of this type, as are agendas that arise out of a request to divide the question. A *uniform partition agenda* is necessarily symmetric, and any such agenda can represent a bill-by-bill (or Plott–Levine) agenda, given an appropriate labelling of alternatives. However, once alternatives are labelled, only a subset of such agendas are admissible bill-by-bill agendas.[10]

More or less the polar opposite of a partition agenda is a *pairwise agenda*, i.e, a binary agenda such that, for every non-initial node v, the surviving set $\Gamma'(v)$ is a one-element set. At each decision node, therefore, two challenged alternatives are paired for a vote. The informal specification of agendas

---

[10]For example, given the labelling of alternatives in Agenda Example 7, the two admissible variants are shown in Figure 6; the inadmissible variant has $\Gamma(v_0)=\{x,v\}$ and $\Gamma(v_1)=\{y,z\}$. Given three or more questions, 'conditional' bill-by-bill agendas can also be devised, such that the order in which later questions are taken up depends on the result of earlier votes.

presented in the previous subsection (in terms of 'x vs. y' or 'winner at vote 2 vs. z') is therefore fully adequate for pairwise agendas but entailed problems (noted in connection with Agenda Examples 6 and 7) for non-pairwise agendas.[11] Every pairwise agenda is complete and every complete non-repetitive agenda is pairwise. Therefore every pairwise agenda is uniform, invariably requiring exactly $k - 1$ votes. Amendment agendas are pairwise, as are their discontinuous (two-stage or multi-stage, conditional or unconditional) variants.

Finally, a *standard* agenda is one in which at every outcome node follows a final decision node v such that $\Gamma(v)$ is a two-element set $\{x, x_0\}$, where x_0 is the status quo. Put substantively, a standard agenda invariably entails a final vote against the status quo. Backward-built amendment agendas are standard but forward-built ones are not. Successive, sequential, and bill-by-bill agendas are not standard. An agenda with compatible amendments (such as Agenda Example 6) is in effect a bill-by-bill agenda 'standardized' by a final vote against the status quo.

An agenda tree does not fully specify a voting procedure, for it does not indicate how votes are cast and counted at each node to determine which following node the voting process will reach. A complete specification of a sequential binary voting procedure, therefore, is a binary agenda tree in conjunction with a vote counting rule assigned to each decision node of the tree. Unless otherwise noted, we assume that the standard parliamentary vote counting rule (the resolute variant of relative majority rule) is assigned to every decision node.[12]

3. VOTER PREFERENCES

Having considered various types of voting agendas, we now turn to the preferences of committee members. In this section we briefly review standard notation and assumptions, introduce several rather natural restrictions

---

[11] Ordeshook and Schwartz (1987) in effect define an agenda as a binary agenda tree together with a function that assigns a unique alternative to each non-initial node. The substantive supposition behind their definition is that all binary agendas are effectively pairwise, but this supposition seems hard to justify.

[12] In general, different vote counting rules can be assigned to different decision nodes of an agenda tree. An example is provided by voting on treaties, constitutional amendments, or other special legislation in the U.S. Congress, where a two-thirds majority is required on final passage but earlier votes on proposed amendments are taken on the basis of simple majority rule.

on preferences, and consider properties of the collective preferences of the whole committee.

3.1. Preference Orderings

Formally, we specify voter preferences by considering the set X of *alternatives* and postulating a set of *preference relations*, one for each voter, over these alternatives. (Note that preferences are defined over alternatives, not the proposals that generate alternatives.) Preferences are defined over the whole set X of alternatives and, *a fortiori*, over the subset A of alternatives actually on the agenda. A *preference profile* is a collection of preference relations, one for each voter.

Let R_i designate the preference relation of voter i, a member of the set $N = \{1, 2, \ldots, n\}$ of all voters. By $x R_i y$, we mean that voter i regards alternative x as at least as good as alternative y. Pursuant to standard theory, we assume that each preference relation R_i is: (i) *reflexive*, i.e., for every x in X, $x R_i x$; (ii) *complete*, i.e., for every x and y in X, either $x R_i y$ or $y R_i x$; and (iii) *transitive*, i.e., for every x, y, and z in X such that $x R_i y$ and $y R_i z$, it is true that $x R_i z$. These assumptions together imply that each R_i is a *weak ordering*.

Each R_i can be factored into its *asymmetric* and *symmetric* components, respectively: (1) i *strictly prefers* x to y if $x R_i y$ *and not* $y R_i x$, which we write $x P_i y$; and (2) i is *indifferent* between x and y if $x R_i y$ *and* $y R_i x$, which we write $x I_i y$. If a voter i is never indifferent between distinct alternatives, his preferences are *strong*, and R_i is a *strong ordering*. In most of what follows, we assume voters have strong preferences, in particular over alternatives in the agenda set A.

We introduce this further terminology and notation: for every alternative x in X, voter i has a (strict) *preference set* $P_i(x) = \{y$ in X such that $y P_i x\}$ and an *inverse preference set* $P_i^{-1}(x) = \{y$ in X such that $x P_i y\}$. We analogously define his *indifference set* $I_i(x)$, *weak preference set* $R_i(x)$, and *inverse weak preference set* $R_i^{-1}(x)$. (Such preference sets may also be defined with respect to specified subsets of X, most notably the agenda set A.) The set of voter i's most preferred alternatives in any subset X' of alternatives is called his *choice set* $C_i(X')$ from X'.

If voter i's preference relation is an ordering, it can also be described by an *ordinal utility function* u_i, which assigns a real number to each element of X such that $u_i(x) \geq u_i(y)$ if and only if $x R_i y$.

Thus far, our assumptions about preferences imply simply that each voter has a preference ordering over alternatives. But we can define certain restrictions on preferences (or preference profiles) that have natural interpretations in that they model, in at least stylized ways, different contexts of political choice and that also have significant consequences when we examine collective preferences and voting outcomes.

3.2. Single-Peaked Preferences

Suppose that a committee must decide on the funding level of some collective activity, or the level of provision of some *public good*, and that three proposals have been offered:

x :   fund at \$1 million;
y :   fund at \$2 million; and
z :   fund at \$3 million.

It *may* be plausible to suppose that, in this case, voter preferences would be structured in this fashion: any voter who most prefers x would also prefer y to z, and any voter who most prefers z would also prefer y to x. The notion is that a voter who most prefers the lowest funding level would, given a choice between two funding levels he considers higher than optimal, prefer the lower of these, and conversely for a voter who most prefers the highest funding level.[13] Similar considerations follow if x, y, and z are policies (or candidates, etc.) commonly perceived in the following *ideological* fashion:

x :   the leftwing alternative;
y :   the centrist alternative; and
z :   the rightwing alternative.

In either event, the upshot is that, while six distinct strong orderings of three alternatives are logically possible, under circumstances such as those described we might expect to find at most four of the six ordering actually held by voters, as shown below.

---

[13] It should be emphasized that single-peakedness, while often plausible, does not derive as a logical necessity from a commonly perceived dimension. For example, a voter who most prefers a high funding level for a program may also believe that, in the event such funding is not provided, little or no funding would be preferable to an intermediate amount that would not accomplish its purpose.

Low Funding/ Leftist	Middle Funding/ Centrist		High Funding/ Rightist	Inadmissible	
x	y	y	z	x	z
y	x	z	y	z	x
z	z	x	x	y	y

The crucial point is that y is perceived by all voters as the alternative that lies 'between' the other two on the relevant evaluative dimension, so nobody ranks y lowest in preference.

This structuring of preferences is called — following Black (1948 and 1958) — *single peakedness*, for reasons that will become clear in the next subsection. Formally, voter preferences over a finite set of alternatives are *single-peaked* if (i) there are just two alternatives or (ii) there is a strong ordering S of the set of three or more alternatives such that, for every x, y, and z in the set of alternatives such that y lies between x and z in S, either $y \, P_i x$ or $y \, P_i z$ (or both) for every voter i. Substantively, the strong ordering S referred to in the definition is the commonly perceived evaluative dimension such that y lies between x and z on this dimension. The intuitive notion is that each voter has a most preferred alternative and, with respect to all alternatives that lie to one side of his most preferred alternative on this dimension, the voter prefers the alternative closer to his most preferred alternative to the more distant alternative, and likewise for all alternatives that lie to the other side of his most preferred alternative.

3.3. Spatial Preferences

To this point, we have assumed that the set X of alternatives is a finite set of discrete alternatives. Indeed, the agenda set A of alternatives that a committee actually votes on must be finite and, in practice, quite small. But often it is plausible to think of A as drawn out of a much larger, possibly infinite, set X of (potential) alternatives. Especially as we consider agenda formation, we shall want to describe preferences over this larger alternative set.

It is often natural to think of this larger set as an *alternative space* of one or more dimensions. Consider the example we used to introduce the notion of single-peakedness. There were three alternatives, x, y, and z, which represented different funding levels for a particular project. These three funding levels presumably had been proposed as explicit motions to be voted on. But the 'space' of possible funding levels is much larger — indeed, it is essentially a continuum including an infinite number of alternatives. And we may suppose that each voter has preferences over the entire continuum. What 'shape' might these preferences have and how might we describe them?

Consider a one-dimensional space X, represented by a horizontal line, every point x on which represents a potential alternative. (In the spatial context, we will generally use the term 'point,' rather than 'potential alternative.') We can then use the vertical dimension to represent levels of utility and draw voters' utility functions above the horizontal line. Now the question is: what might be the general shape of such utility functions?

First, we might expect that the utility function of any voter i achieves its maximum at a unique point, i.e., i's most preferred point x^{i^*} on the alternative continuum. We call x^{i^*} voter i's *ideal point*. Second, we might expect that, on either side of this maximum, $u_i(x)$ strictly declines with distance from x^{i^*}. Thus a curve representing the utility function is literally *single-peaked* — as we look across the alternative continuum, the curve rises without interruption until it reaches its highest point and then it declines without interruption.[14] Thus the notion of single-peakedness applied to an continuum of alternatives is a natural generalization of the notion of single-peakedness applied to discrete alternatives.

A more stringent restriction is that the dependence of preference on distance from ideal point holds, not only for points on the same side of the ideal point, but also for points on opposite sides. In this event, the utility curve is symmetric about its maximum, and we say preferences are *symmetric single-peaked*. Given symmetric single-peakedness, a voter's (ordinal) preferences are fully specified by the location of his ideal point.

We have considered preferences over possible funding levels for a single project. Now suppose we have a second project (or a multiplicity of other projects) that may be funded at any level. The result is a two-dimensional (or multidimensional) space of (potential) alternatives. Or each dimension in a multidimensional space may correspond to an issue with a continuum of positions. Or the space may represent the several ideological dimensions (e.g., left-to-right on economic issues, left-to-right on social issues, etc.) in

---

[14] Technically, we should also assume that utility functions nowhere 'jump' up or down, i.e., that they are *continuous*, and that (if the space is unbounded), for every point x distinct from x^{i^*}, there is another point x' on the opposite side of x^{i^*} such that $u_i(x)=u_i(x')$, i.e., that preferences are *compact*.

terms of which policies are commonly perceived and differently evaluated. Most generally, the multidimensional framework provides a general way of representing a notion of 'distance' between alternatives.

What then might be the shape of voter utility functions defined over a space of two (or more) dimensions? Based on the considerations previously outlined, we might expect any voter i's preferences over the points on any straight line through the space (called his *induced preferences* on the line) to be single-peaked. We refer to such preferences as *standard spatial preferences*.

Given an alternative space of two dimensions, we cannot draw a complete utility function, but we can sketch in selected *indifference curves* for any voter i; these lines are simply the indifference sets $I_i(x)$ for selected points x. Given standard spatial voter preferences: (1) preference sets are strictly convex, so indifference curves are nested about the voter's ideal point and are everywhere curving 'inward' toward it; and (2) indifference sets are *thin*, i.e., (curved) lines with no interior.[15] Illustrative indifference curves are shown in Figure 9.

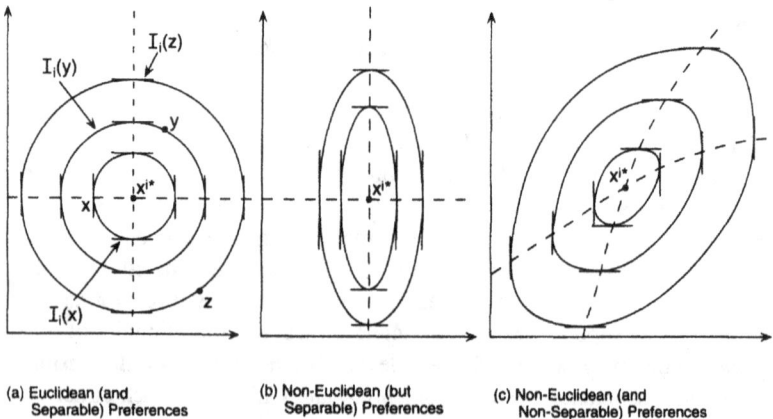

(a) Euclidean (and Separable) Preferences

(b) Non-Euclidean (but Separable) Preferences

(c) Non-Euclidean (and Non-Separable) Preferences

FIGURE 9 Spatial Preferences

[15]Further, from continuity, it follows that indifference curves exist and are unbroken, and from compactness, it follows that they are closed curves. Finally, it is ordinarily assumed that indifference curves are smooth, so that there is a single line tangent to an indifference curve at any point. In higher dimensional alternative spaces, indifference curves become surfaces (or hypersurfaces).

One variant of standard spatial preferences is especially simple and analytically tractable. A voter has *Euclidean* preferences if his preferences are based strictly on Euclidean distance, i.e. if, in comparing any two points in the space, he prefers the point closer to his ideal point to the point more distant from his ideal and is indifferent between points equidistant from his ideal. (This generalizes symmetric single-peakedness to two or more dimensions.) Thus, in a two-dimensional space, the indifference curves of a voter with Euclidean preferences are concentric circles centered on the voters ideal point, as shown in Figure 9(a). Non-Euclidean standard spatial preferences are illustrated in Figures 9(b) and 9(c).

3.4. Separable Preferences

Suppose a committee is considering a number of distinct 'bills' (or 'issues,' 'projects,' etc.) under a bill-by-bill or issue-by-issue agenda. Each bill comprises a set of *positions* — certainly at least two, e.g., 'passage' and 'defeat,' and perhaps more, e.g., passage of the bill with different amendments attached. The set of alternatives from which the committee must ultimately choose is the set of all possible combinations of positions, one from each bill.

When we consider voter preferences with respect to these alternatives, it *may* be plausible to suppose that only certain orderings of the combinations will actually occur. Consider the simplest case in which there are just two bills A and B, and each has just two positions, a_1 and a_2 and b_1 and b_2, respectively. The set X of alternatives is therefore the *Cartesian product* $X = A \times B = \{(a_1, b_1), (a_1, b_2), (a_2, b_1), (a_2, b_2)\}$. There are 24 possible strong orderings of four alternatives, but — considering the particular composition of these alternatives — we might suppose that only a subset of eight will actually occur in the preferences of the committee.

In particular, suppose that each voter has preferences over the positions on each issue that are independent of the other issue. The name given to this sometimes plausible assumption is *separability*. For example, voter i may prefer position a_1 to a_2 on A, regardless of the outcome on issue B, and he may likewise prefer b_2 to b_1 on B. Thus i's most preferred alternative is (a_1, b_2) and his least preferred alternative is (a_2, b_1). A specification of a voter's preferences over *positions on issues* does not fully specify his preferences over *alternatives*, for it is not apparent what i's preference might be between (a_1, b_2) and (a_2, b_1). This choice poses to voter i the question:

'If you could get your way on just one of the two issues, which one would it be?' Given this domain of alternatives, there are eight strong orderings that are consistent with separability since each voter may prefer a_1 to a_2 or *vice versa*, prefer b_1 to b_2 or *vice versa*, and prefer to get his way on issue A rather than issue B (in the event he can get his way on only one) or *vice versa*. There are, of course, an additional sixteen logically possible strong orderings of four alternatives, but they are inadmissible given separability.

A special case of particular relevance is that in which issues or bills are *dichotomous*, i.e., have just two positions (as was the case in the earlier illustrative example and in the examples of bill-by-bill agendas in the previous section). Given an odd number of voters with strong separable preferences, the two positions on each issue can be designated the *majority position* and *minority position*; according to their respective support.

The notion of separability applies to multidimensional spatial preferences, given orthogonal axes defining the dimensions of the space and where each dimension represents an 'issue.' Consider the two-dimensional examples in Figure 9. We can trace out the locus of the voter's induced ideal points (shown by dotted lines) on one dimension as positions on the other vary. The preferences in Figures 9(a) and 9(b) are separable, as each locus of induced ideal points is a straightline passing through the voter's ideal point and orthogonal to the corresponding issue dimension. On the other hand, the preferences in Figure 9(c) are non-separable.

3.5. Particularistic Preferences

To this point, our discussion of restrictions on preferences has essentially assumed that alternatives are in the nature of proposed levels of provision of one or more *public goods* or are located in one or more *ideological* dimensions. But sometimes alternatives confronting a committee are, in effect, proposed allocations among the voters (or — if the voters are legislative representatives — among their constituencies, which will induce similar preferences among legislators motivated to please their constituents) of some divisible and essentially *private good*, or the parcelling out among voters (or their constituencies) of particularized benefits (such as public works projects), the costs of which are shared by all. This pattern of political decision making is commonly referred to as 'pork-barrel politics' in the American context, and the term 'distributive politics' is widely used in academic political science. Clearly this political context structures preference profiles in a distinctive manner but not in the 'ideological' manner of spatial preferences. Here we present two stylized representations of such *particularistic* preferences. The simplest formulation is as follows. Each alternative corresponds to some allocation of a fixed amount of a divisible good. Such an allocation q may be described by vector of non-negative numbers $< q_1, q_2, \ldots, q_n >$, where each q_i is the share of the good received by voter i and the q_is add up to no more than some constant amount K (the total amount of the good). Then we might suppose that $q \, R_i q'$ if and only if $q_i \geq q'_i$. Such preferences are called *individualistic*.

Individualistic preferences assume, in effect, that the good is exogenously provided — there is no cost of provision which must also be allocated among voters. Another formalization, which we present in its discrete variant, incorporates such costs. Suppose a committee of n members is considering n distinct issues, each of which concerns whether or not a 'project,' which will provide benefits exclusively to an individual voter i (or his constituents), should be publicly funded. While the benefit b_i of each project is concentrated in this fashion, the cost c_i is shared by all voters (or their constituents). For convenience, let us suppose that costs are shared equally, so that each voter bears a cost of c_i/n if the i [th] project is funded. This provides the basis for a simple model of 'distributive' or 'pork barrel' politics — generally the politics of particularized benefits and generalized costs, which seems to be an important feature of legislative bodies, especially those elected from single-member districts. An alternative x is a *project package* that may be described by a vector of n numbers $< p_1, \ldots, p_n >$, the i [th] entry of which is 1 if voter i's project is provided and is 0 otherwise. Then, given *distributive preferences*, each voter evaluates packages in terms of the benefits it provides him net of his share of the costs, i.e., $u_i(x) = b_i p_i - (\sum c_j p_j)/n$.

3.6. Collective Preferences

Having examined individual voter preferences, we next consider collective preferences derived from preference profiles and, in particular, majority preference. The unsubscripted symbol R designates a *collective preference relation*, just as the subscripted symbol R_i designates the individual preference relation of voter i. We shall usually say 'x beats y' for $x P y$ and 'x ties y' for $x I y$.

Suppose we have a preference profile over the set X of alternatives. For any pair of alternatives x and y in X, we can partition the set of voters into three subsets: those who prefer x to y, those who prefer y to x, and those who are indifferent between x and y. Given our concern with committee voting and given that vote counting rules are typically anonymous, our concern is primarily with *how many* voters are in each of the three sets; let these numbers be given by $n(x \succ y)$, $n(y \succ x)$, and $n(x = y)$, respectively. And given that the standard parliamentary vote counting rule is a variant of majority rule, we are particularly concerned with whether a *majority* of voters prefers x to y or prefer y to x. If a particular set M of voters all prefer x to y, we say 'x beats y through the coalition M'.

We can define a variety of (anonymous) *collective preference relations* in a fashion directly parallel to our discussion of vote counting rules in 1.2, with *preferences* substituted for *votes*. Let $n' = n(x \succ y) + n(y \succ x)$ be the number of *concerned* voters, not indifferent between x and y. *Relative majority preference* can be defined as follows:

$$x P y \quad \text{if and only if } n(x \succ y) > n'/2;$$
$$y P x \quad \text{if and only if } n(y \succ x) > n'2; \text{ and}$$
$$x I y \quad \text{if and only if } n(x \succ y) = n(y \succ x) = n'/2.$$

Absolute majority preference can be defined as follows:

$$x P y \quad \text{if and only if } n(x \succ y) > n/2;$$
$$y P x \quad \text{if and only if } n(y \succ x) > n/2; \text{ and}$$
$$x I y \quad \text{otherwise.}$$

The two variants of majority preference are equivalent in the event voter preferences are strong.

Relative (or absolute) majority preference is a limiting case of general relative (or absolute) *d-majority (or supra-majority) preference*, which, for any d such that $.5 < d \leq 1$, can be defined as follows:

$$x P y \quad \text{if and only if } n(x \succ y) \geq d \times n' (\text{or } d \times n);$$
$$y P x \quad \text{if and only if } n(y \succ x) \geq d \times n' (\text{or } d \times n); \text{ and}$$
$$x I y \quad \text{otherwise.}$$

As d approaches on its lower limit of .5, we get simple majority preference. With $d = 1$, we have the *unanimous preference relation*. In welfare economics and social choice theory, the asymmetric component of the unanimous preference relation, usually employed in its relative version, is commonly called the *Pareto relation*. Alternatives that are maximal with respect to the Pareto relation are *Pareto-optimal*, and we designate by *PO(X)* the subset of all Pareto-optimal alternatives in X. Thus, if and only if x belongs to *PO(X)*, for any other y in X, such that $y P_i x$ for some voter i, there is some other voter j such that $x P_j y$.

Given any social preference relation R, we can define collective preference sets analogous to individual preference sets introduced in Section 2.1. Thus, $P(x)$ — sometimes called the *win set* of x — is the set of all alternatives in X that beat x. $R(x)$, $I(x)$, $P^{-1}(x)$, and $R^{-1}(x)$ are defined in parallel manner. It is convenient to define $\bar{P}(x)$ as the union of $P(x)$ and $\{x\}$.

A collective preference relation, though derived from individual preference orderings, in general is not itself an ordering. In fact, *McGarvey's* (1953) *Theorem* says this: *if we take any finite set X of alternatives and specify any arbitrary collective preference relation R over these alternatives, we can find some finite profile of strong voter preferences such that R derives from this profile as the majority preference relation.*[16]

To better grasp the import of this result, let us introduce a diagrammatic device that will prove more generally useful. Recall the discussion of *directed graphs* from 2.3. Any preference relation over a set of alternatives may be represented (in one of several ways) by a directed graph. In any such a representation, each *node* corresponds to an *alternative* and each *one-way arrow* represents a *strict preference relationship*. We will follow these additional conventions: an arrow from x to y represents the strict preference relationship $x P y$, and the absence of an arrow between x and y indicates the indifference relationship $x I y$.[17] Thus any preference relation may be represented by a directed graph that is asymmetric but (in general)

---

[16]For each pair of alternatives between which there is strict social preference, say $x P y$, let there be a pair of voters who both prefer x to y but who have opposite preferences with respect to every other pair of alternatives. Then we have altogether twice as many voters as there are strict social preference relationships, and these voters have strong preference orderings such that: (a) for each pair of alternatives between which there is strict social preference, the preferences of all but two of the voters balance out and the common preference of the two remaining voters determines (relative or absolute) majority preference in the required manner; and (b) for each pair of points between which there is social indifference, the preference of all voters balance out, resulting in a tie.

[17]The reader should be warned that some works use the opposite diagrammatic convention and represent $x P y$ by an arrow from y to x. Less confusingly, $x I y$ is sometimes represented by an undirected line (a line with no arrows) or by arrows in both directions.

incomplete; a strong preference relation is represented by a *tournament*, i.e., by a directed graph that is both asymmetric and complete. A directed graph is a redundant way to represent an ordering but is a convenient way to represent a collective preference relation, precisely because it may fail to be an ordering. Indeed, McGarvey's Theorem says that *every* asymmetric digraph represents some majority preference relation.

Because collective preference is not an ordering, an alternative x that fails to beat y may nevertheless 'indirectly beat' y — that is, there may be a collective preference path from x to y. We let $\mathcal{P}(x)$ designate the set of alternatives from which x is reachable by a collective preference path; clearly $\mathcal{P}(x)$ is a superset of $P(x)$ but is empty if $P(x)$ is empty. Again it is convenient to let $\bar{\mathcal{P}}(x)$ designate the union of $\mathcal{P}(x)$ together with $\{x\}$.

We introduce a few more graph-theoretical definitions. A *complete path* in X is a path that includes every alternative in X; if there is a complete path ending with z, $\bar{\mathcal{P}}(z) = X$. A *cycle* is a path of three or more steps from an alternative back to itself; clearly all points in a cycle are mutually reachable. A *complete cycle* in X is a cycle that includes every alternative in X; if there is a complete cycle, $\bar{\mathcal{P}}(x) = X$ for all x in X. A directed graph is *strong* if all points in it are mutually reachable; it follows that a directed graph with a complete cycle is strong, and a strong tournament contains a complete cycle. A subset X' in X is *externally stable* in X if, for every alternative z in $X - X'$, there is some x in X' such that xPz.

It follows from McGarvey's Theorem that majority preference may generate intransitivities and even *cycles*, e.g., $xPyPzPx$. This phenomenon has been called the 'paradox of voting,' the 'Condorcet effect,' the 'Arrow problem,' 'cyclical majorities,' among other appellations. It evidently was first discovered by Condorcet, and it was then alternately forgotten and rediscovered until the work of Black (1948) and Arrow (1951). Cyclical majority preference is most readily illustrated by the following three-voter three-alternative example.[18]

---

[18] Weak majority preference can violate transitivity in less radical ways. For example, given weak individual orderings, we may get xPy and yPz but xIz; and, given an even number of voters, we may get xIy and yIz but yPz. But in a tournament, any failure of transitivity implies cycles.

EXAMPLE 1

<u>Preference Profile</u>   <u>Majority Preference Tournament</u>

1	2	3
x	y	z
y	z	x
z	x	y

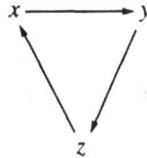

Collective preference intransitivity arises because different collective preference relationships may be effected by different subsets of voters. Under supra-majority rule, as the decision rule d increases, collective preference relationships are converted into collective indifference and in due course cycles disappear.[19] But cycles disappear entirely only when $d = 1$.

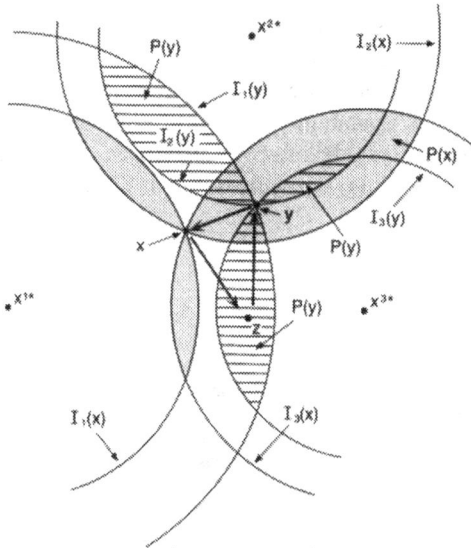

FIGURE 10 Win Sets in Two Dimensions and a Majority Preference Cycle

---

[19] In general, cycles of length m or less are precluded if d exceeds $(m-1)/m$; see Craven (1971) and Ferejohn and Grether (1974).

The question arises of whether we can specify general conditions on preference profiles under which intransitivities of majority preference do, and do not, occur. In particular, what are the implications for collective preference cycles of the restrictions on preferences discussed earlier? It is fundamental that single peakedness precludes cycles in majority preference. Indeed, if the number of voters is odd, single peakedness assures that majority preference is fully transitive (Black, 1948 and 1958; Arrow, 1951). But in two or more dimensions, cycles of majority preference can easily be generated. For example, Figure 10 shows the win set $P(x)$ given three voters with Euclidean preferences. If we consider some point y that beats x, it is not necessarily true that $P(y)$ is contained in $P(x)$. Thus we can often find some point such as z that belongs to both $P(y)$ and $P^{-1}(x)$. As a result, we can construct a cycle such as $xPzPyPx$.

Separable preferences with two or more issues also are likely to entail collective preference cycles. Recall that separability implies we can specify individual preference ordering over positions on issues. Thus, we can straightforwardly derive collective preferences over positions on issues. And if individual preferences are separable, so are collective preferences. Next, any cycle that exists with respect to positions on any single issue (or subset of issues) is, given separability, inherited by collective preferences over alternatives. Finally, even if collective preference over each issue is acyclic, cycles may exist over the alternatives, as is illustrated by the following example.[20]

---

[20] Voters 1 and 2 could, consistent with the assumption of separable preferences, both prefer (a_1, b_1) to (a_2, b_2), in which case collective preference would be fully transitive. In the latter event, it can be said that voter 1 and voter 2 each prefers to get his way on the issue with respect to which he prefers the more popular position (if he can get his way on only one issue). On the other hand, given the preference profile displayed in Example 2, it can be said that voter 1 and voter 2 each prefers to get his way on the issue with respect to which he prefers the less popular position. But the two voters together constitute a majority coalition and thus can form an effective 'coalition of minorities' in support of a 'logrolling agreement' to secure the alternative that includes, for each voter, his more preferred position on the issue he cares more about. An early result in the theory of voting, provided independently and more or less simultaneously by many different researchers, e.g., Kadane (1972), Oppenheimer (1972), Bernholz (1973 and 1974), Miller (1975), Koehler (1975), Schwartz (1977), was this demonstration that an effective coalition of minorities entails cyclical social preference; for a general review, see Miller (1977a).

EXAMPLE 2

Preference Profile	Majority Preference Tournament

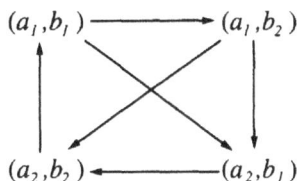

Preference Profile

$\underline{1}$	$\underline{2}$	$\underline{3}$
(a_2,b_1)	(a_1,b_2)	(a_1,b_1)
(a_2,b_2)	(a_2,b_2)	(a_1,b_2)
(a_1,b_1)	(a_1,b_1)	(a_2,b_1)
(a_1,b_2)	(a_2,b_1)	(a_2,b_2)

Majority Preference Tournament

$(a_1,b_1) \longrightarrow (a_1,b_2)$

$(a_2,b_2) \longleftarrow (a_2,b_1)$

Cycles are also pervasive in the distributive context. Given pure allocation, for almost every pair of efficient allocations q' and q'' such that $q'Pq''$, there is a third allocation q^* such that $q^*Pq'Pq''Pq^*$ (Epstein, 1992). In the simple distributive case in which each proposed 'project' provides the same benefit b at the same shared cost c, majority preference is fully transitive if and only if $b \le c/n$ — that is when and only when the benefit provided each voter is less that his share of the cost — and three-alternative majority preference cycles are precluded if and only if $b \le 2c/n$. A more equal (and plausible) balance between benefits and costs, or a moderately large voting body, entails highly intransitive majority preference (see Weingast, 1979; Shepsle and Weingast, 1981, Miller, 1982).

4. VOTING BEHAVIOR

We have examined voting agendas, which together with vote counting rules, fix a 'game form' or, in more substantive language, an *institutional structure* for voting. We have examined voter preferences, which fix the *motivations of the voters*. These two ingredients give us a *voting game*, and we aim to identify the 'solution,' i.e., the voting outcome, for any voting game. But in order to do this, we must make some *behavioral assumption* concerning the actions of individual voters. Three principal categories of behavior have been employed in developing the theory of voting.

The first is that voters behave *non-strategically* — that is, they take no account of the preferences or likely behavior of other voters. By far the most common assumption within this general category is that of *sincere voting* — that voters vote 'honestly.' The assumption of sincere behavior may be reasonable if voters are uninformed about each others' preferences.

The second category is that voters make their choices *strategically* — that is, they take account of the preferences and likely behavior of others — but in *isolation* from one another. The standard assumption within this category is that of *sophisticated voting* — that voters behave in a strategically optimal fashion in the sense of non-cooperative game theory. The assumption of sophisticated behavior is reasonable if voters are informed about each other's preferences but cannot make enforceable agreements among themselves.

The third category is that voters make their choices *strategically* and in *collaboration* with one another. The general assumption within this category is that of *cooperative voting* — that voters enter into coalitions and coordinate their voting in an optimal fashion in the sense of cooperative game theory. The assumption of cooperative behavior is reasonable if voters can enter into agreements which can be effectively monitored and enforced or are otherwise trustworthy.

In order to describe these behavioral assumptions precisely, we need to introduce the notion of a 'voting strategy.' In doing this, we use ordinary game theory concepts in conjunction with some terminology introduced by Farquharson (1969a).

4.1. Voting Strategies

In general, a *strategy* for a player is a complete plan of action for playing a game, making use of whatever information may be available. So a *voting strategy* is a complete plan of action for casting votes in the voting game determined by a particular agenda and applicable vote counting rules. The *strategy set* of a voter is the set of all his strategies.

Given a sequential binary procedure (and ignoring the possibility of abstention), a voter i has exactly two possible actions at each decision node v: a vote of $V_i = +1$ ('yes' or for node v_1) or $V_i = -1$ ('no' or for node v_0). A voting strategy specifies a vote at every decision node and may be written as a sequences of $+1$s and -1s, one number for each decision node in some specified order. Thus, given a binary voting agenda with k decision nodes, each voter has a strategy set of 2^k voting strategies.

A *situation* is a strategy n-tuple, one for each voter. Any situation determines a *voting path* through the agenda tree from the initial decision node to some outcome node, and thus also determines a voting outcome; as a shortcut, we say a situation *gives* a particular outcome. A *contingency* for voter i is a strategy $(n - 1)$-tuple, one for each voter other than i. Thus a strategy for voter i in conjunction with a contingency for i is a situation; again as a shortcut, we say that a strategy *gives* a particular outcome in a given contingency. A *game form* is a function that maps situations into outcomes. A *voting game form* reflects the *agenda structure* and the *vote counting rule* used at each decision node and thus formally represents the institutional structure of voting. A game form is commonly presented as an array, each dimension (set of rows, columns, etc.) of which represents the strategy set of one player; each element of the array is the outcome given by the corresponding situation.

Let us illustrate these concepts by means of the simplest possible non-trivial case of sequential binary voting. Figure 11(a) shows the nodes of the agenda tree for the case of successive procedure with three alternatives, in the manner of Figure 1. Figure 11(b) shows the nodes identified by their reachable sets, in the manner of Figures 2–8. Since there are two decision nodes, each voter has four strategies, which we label in terms of the choices they prescribe at v and v_1, respectively, as follows:

$$s^1 = (-1, -1); \qquad s^3 = (+1, -1); \quad \text{and}$$
$$s^2 = (-1, +1); \qquad s^4 = (+1, +1).$$

We label strategy s^h, when selected by voter i, s_i^h.

Given three voters, the game form maps the $4^3 = 64$ distinct situations into outcomes according to the agenda structure and vote counting rule at each decision node. Given majority rule at both nodes, the game form is that displayed in Figure 11(c) in an (attempted) three-dimensional representation. Figure 11(d) shows the same game form after the following manipulation has been performed: the $4 \times 4 \times 4$ array has been rearranged into a two-dimensional 4×16 matrix by combining strategies, one for each of two voters, into contingencies for the third.

In Figures 11(c) and 11(d) and in the discussion up to now, we have folded the entire voting process into a single stage (called the *normal* or *strategic form* in game theory), so that each voter appears to be making a single decision, i.e., selecting a voting strategy. For many purposes however, it is more enlightening to take explicit account of the multistage or sequential structure of committee voting. From this point of view, we may think of any voting game form under sequential binary procedure as composed of a hierarchy of *subgame forms*, one at each

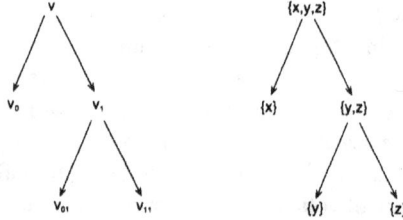

(a) The Agenda Tree for Successive Procedure with Three Alternatives

(b) Reachable Sets For Successive Procedure with Three Alternatives

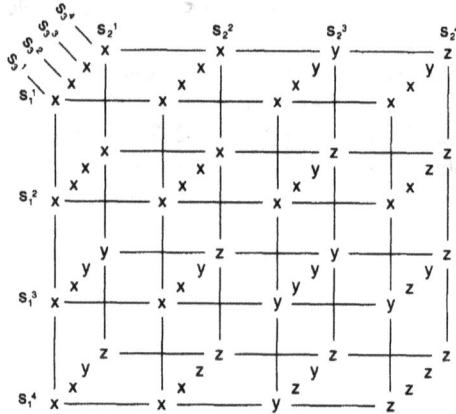

(c) The Game Form for Successive Procedure with Three Alternatives

contingencies

strategies	1 S^1,S^1	2 S^1,S^2	3 S^1,S^3	4 S^1,S^4	5 S^2S^1	6 S^2S^2	7 S^2S^3	8 S^2S^4	9 S^3S^1	10 S^3S^2	11 S^3S^3	12 S^3S^4	13 S^4S^1	14 S^4S^2	15 S^4S^3	16 S^4S^4
S^1	x	x	x	x	x	x	x	x	x	x	y	y	x	x	y	z
S^2	x	x	x	x	x	x	x	x	x	x	y	z	x	x	z	z
S^3	x	x	y	y	x	x	y	z	y	y	y	y	y	z	y	z
S^4	x	x	y	z	x	x	z	z	y	z	z	z	z	z	z	z

(d) The Rearranged Game Form

FIGURE 11 Successive Procedure with Three Alternatives

decision node and each with just two possible outcomes. Each subgame form represents the vote counting rule assigned to that node. The agenda structure determines how these subgame forms are sequenced. A subgame form associated with a final decision node has alternatives as outcomes. A subgame form associated with a non-final decision node has other subgame forms as outcomes (or perhaps, if the agenda is non-uniform, a subgame form as one outcome and an alternative as the other).

The motivation of a voter in such a subgame is determined, as always, by his preferences over outcomes. At a subgame associated with a final decision node, the possible outcomes are two alternatives from the set over which voter preferences are defined, so voter preferences are clear. At a subgame associated with a non-final decision node, one or both outcomes are other subgames. A voter has a preference between these subgames induced by his preferences over alternatives, in conjunction with his expectations concerning how the final outcome will be different according to whether one or other subgame is next played. These expectations may be formed under different behavioral assumptions. It is these behavioral assumptions that distinguish, in particular, 'sincere' from 'strategic' voting behavior.

4.2. Sincere Voting Behavior

Black (1958: p. 5) assumed that committee members vote 'in accordance with their schedules of preference'; in Farquharson's more succinct (and now standard) terminology, Black assumed that voting is 'sincere.'

If alternatives are explicitly paired for votes, the notion of sincere voting is intuitively clear, at least for a voter with strong preferences: a sincere voter always votes for his more preferred alternative. But not all agendas are pairwise (or even binary). For non-repetitive sequential binary procedures, Farquharson (1969a) developed the following notion of sincerity: a sincere voter has (often excessively) 'optimistic' expectations, always aiming for the best possible outcome; specifically, in choosing at node v between the two subgames associated with nodes v_0 and v_1, a sincere voter prefers, and votes for, the subgame associated with the node whose best reachable outcome from among the alternatives challenged at v he prefers. Put more formally, at decision node v, a sincere voter i looks at the possible outcomes in $\Gamma'(v_0)$ and $\Gamma'(v_1)$ associated with each following node, identifies the best alternative(s) in each, i.e., his choice sets at $C_i[\Gamma'(v_0)]$ and $C_i[\Gamma'(v_1)]$, and votes for v_0 or v_1 according to whether $x P_i y$ or $y P_i x$ for x in $C_i[\Gamma'(v_0)]$

and y in $C_i[\Gamma'(v_1)]$.[21] This defines a *sincere voting choice* at any decision node. A *sincere voting strategy* is one that prescribes a sincere voting choice at every decision node. A voter with strong preferences has a unique sincere choice at every decision node and therefore a unique sincere voting strategy.

If this definition of sincere voting seems complex and non-intuitive, we should note that, under any pairwise agenda, it simplifies to the simple and intuitive notion that a sincere voter always votes for his more preferred alternative, for in this case each $\Gamma'(v)$ is a one-element set. In fact, in Black's original discussion (which did not employ any agenda tree apparatus) and in many other discussions, sincere voting is described simply as voting for one's more preferred alternative, on the assumption that all agendas are pairwise.[22]

4.3. Voting Equilibria

Black, and most early students of voting, assumed that all voters were sincere. But many of these early analysts also recognized, at least in an *ad hoc* way, that sincerity is not always expedient. A standard example is that a legislator who opposes a bill might vote for an amendment even though (in his view) it makes the bill even worse, on the calculation that the bill burdened by the amendment will ultimately be defeated, though otherwise it would pass.

Though Black was concerned almost exclusively with sincere voting, he did demonstrate, by means of examples, that under standard amendment procedure, 'it may be open to one or more of the members to bring into existence a decision more favourable to themselves by voting otherwise than in accordance with their schedules of preference' (1958: p. 44). Here is an example using an amendment agenda with three alternatives.

---

[21] If $x I_i y$, Farquharson applies the same rule to the next most preferred challenged alternatives, and so forth.

[22] Ordeshook and Schwartz (1987) define sincere voting differently, in terms of their definition of an agenda tree (see footnote 11). Since a pairwise agenda tree is compatible with only one Ordeshook-Schwartz agenda, the two definitions are equivalent in this case. But if an agenda fails to be pairwise due to incompleteness, the two definitions can label different choices — and thus different strategies — as sincere.

EXAMPLE 3

Preference Profile   Agenda

$$
\begin{array}{ccc}
\underline{1} & \underline{2} & \underline{3} \\
y & x & z \\
x & z & x \\
z & y & y
\end{array}
$$

$$
\begin{array}{c}
\{x,y,z\} \\
\swarrow \qquad \searrow \\
\{x,z\} \qquad\qquad \{y,z\} \\
\swarrow\ \searrow \qquad\quad \swarrow\ \searrow \\
\{x\}\quad\{z\}\qquad \{y\}\quad\{z\}
\end{array}
$$

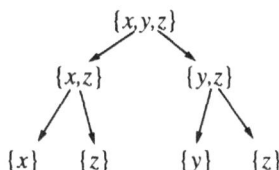

If all voting is sincere, x wins at the first vote with the support of 2 and 3, and x also wins the second vote with the support of 1 and 2. Therefore x is the *sincere voting outcome*. However, if voter 3 were to vote 'insincerely' for y instead of x at the first vote, y would win the first vote with the support of 1 and 3, and z would win at the second vote with the support 2 and 3. Therefore z would be the voting outcome, which voter 3 prefers to y. In this precise sense, sincere voting is inexpedient for 3.

More formal analysis of this example will serve to introduce additional concepts and also help fix in mind concepts and notation already introduced. There are eight distinct voting strategies — each specified by a vector of three -1s and/or $+1$s, prescribing choices at the three decision nodes (labelled as in Figure 1) v, v_0, and v_1, respectively — which we label as follows:

$$
\begin{aligned}
s^1 &= (-1,-1,-1); & s^5 &= (+1,-1,-1); \\
s^2 &= (-1,-1,+1); & s^6 &= (+1,-1,+1); \\
s^3 &= (-1,+1,-1); & s^7 &= (+1,+1,-1); \quad \text{and} \\
s^4 &= (-1,+1,+1); & s^8 &= (+1,+1,+1).
\end{aligned}
$$

(We will not try to construct a game form in the manner Figure 11(c) or 11(d), for we would have an array with $8^3 = 512$ situations.) Voter 1's sincere voting strategy is s^5, 2's is s^2, and 3's is s^4. Thus the *sincere voting situation* is the strategy triple (s_1^5, s_2^2, s_3^4), which gives x as the outcome.

A strategy s_i is a *best reply* for a voter i in contingency t_i in the event no other strategy gives a better outcome in that contingency. A situation is *vulnerable* to voter i if his strategy is not a best reply in that contingency. A voting situation is an *individual voting equilibrium* if it is not vulnerable to any individual voter. In Example 3, the sincere voting situation (s_1^5, s_2^2, s_3^4) is vulnerable to voter 3, since (s_1^5, s_2^2, s_3^8) gives z as the outcome and 3 prefers z to x. This demonstrates that a sincere voting strategy is not always a best reply — not even in the contingency made up entirely of sincere strategies for other voters — and that a sincere voting situation is not always a voting equilibrium.

Many early works took note of examples such as this. But for the most part these works merely noted that there may be an incentive for a voter to vote insincerely; they did not get at the matter of how voters should vote, or what would happen if all voters tried to vote strategically.[23] In like manner, the analysis above identifies a 'strategic move' open to voter 3 but does not consider countermoves that may be open to other voters, or counter-countermoves open to 3 and so forth.

We can, however, pursue analysis of Example 3 a bit further. Suppose voter 3 switches to s^8. Is the new situation (s_1^5, s_2^2, s_3^8) an equilibrium? No, because s^5 is no longer 1's best reply in the new contingency; 1 can benefit by switching to s^1 as (s_1^1, s_2^2, s_3^8) gives x as the outcome, which 1 prefers to z.

We can verify that (s_1^1, s_2^2, s_3^8) is a voting equilibrium, so we might think of it as the 'strategic voting situation.' Indeed, this conclusion would be appropriate in the particular example, but we cannot in general equate voting equilibria with 'strategic voting situations,' for voting games typically possess many equilibria that together give all possible outcomes. While we may expect all 'strategic voting situations' to be equilibria, we cannot expect the reverse to be true.

4.4. Straightforward Voting Strategies

Let us now examine the game form matrix in Figure 11(d) more closely and consider the six possible strong preference orderings of the three alternatives.

R^1	R^2	R^3	R^4	R^5	R^6
x	x	y	y	z	z
y	z	x	z	x	y
z	y	z	x	y	x

---

[23] A few early works, e.g., Grofman (1969), analyzed strategic voting in greater depth but in a substantially *ad hoc* fashion.

Consider a voter who has the ordering R^1. Such a voter's sincere strategy is s^1. Examination of the matrix shows that such a voter would never regret using his sincere strategy. Put otherwise, given this game form and this preference ordering, the strategy s^1 is a best reply in *every contingency*. Such a strategy is commonly called *dominant* and was dubbed *straightforward* by Farquharson (1956, 1969a). A voter with a straightforward strategy has no reason to try to anticipate how other voters will vote since, no matter what they do, he can do no better than select that strategy. A voter with a straightforward strategy certainly is not indifferent to other voters' preferences or what strategies they select, and such a voter may be totally defeated in the sense that the outcome is the alternative he least prefers, but he need never regret his strategy selection.

It may be checked that voters with several other preference orderings also have straightforward strategies in this game form. Not all voters have straightforward strategies, however. A voter with ordering R^3, for example, would regret using his sincere strategy s^3 in contingencies 8 and 14; at the same time, he would regret using each of his other strategies in a number of contingencies. Such a voter must condition his strategy selection on expectations concerning the behavior of other voters. The question thus arises: why do voters with some preference orderings have straightforward strategies while others do not?

Let us consider a committee that is choosing between just two alternatives, x and y, on the basis of some vote counting rule. We establish these conventions; $V_i = -1$ represents a vote for x and $F(V) = -1$ selection of x, and $V_i = +1$ represents a vote for y and $F(V) = +1$ selection of y. In the two-alternative case, a vote is equivalent to a strategy, a vote configuration is equivalent to a situation, and the result given by a vote configuration is equivalent to the outcome given by a situation. Now we have the *Binary Vote Counting Theorem: in a two-alternative voting game form with a non-negatively responsive and resolute vote counting rule, every sincere strategy of every voter i is straightforward.*[24]

---

[24]By resoluteness, contingencies for i may be partitioned into four classes: (1) those that give x as the outcome, regardless of i's vote; (2) those that give y as the outcome, regardless of i's vote; (3) those that give x as the outcome if and only if $V_i = -1$ and give y if and only if $V_i = +1$; and (4) those that give x as the outcome if and only if $V_i = +1$ and give y if and only if $V_i = -1$. By non-negative responsiveness, category (4) is empty. It follows that: (a) if $x P_i y$, strategy (-1) is sincere and a best reply for i in every contingency; (b) if $y P_i x$, strategy $(+1)$ is sincere and a best reply for i in every contingency; and (c) if $x I_i y$, both strategies are (trivially) sincere and best replies in every contingency. (This result also holds if we allow voters to

The upshot, therefore, is that each voter has a straightforward strategy within the subgame associated with each decision node, provided the voter has (so to speak) 'straightforward' preferences between its two possible outcomes. Clearly, each voter does have such preferences at any final decision node, since both outcomes of the subgame form are alternatives. Equally clearly, a voter may not have such preferences at other decision nodes. In particular, the preferences that define a sincere voting choice are not necessarily 'straightforward.' Consider, for example, a voter with the preference ordering R^3 in the example depicted in Figure 11. His sincere strategy is s^3, but this strategy is not straightforward. At the first node, i's sincere choice aims for the node v_1 with his beat reachable alternative y, but this node also has his worst reachable alternative z. Thus such a voter might regret selecting s^3, for the ultimate outcome might be z, whereas, if he had made the opposite choice at the first node and if his vote had been pivotal (as responsiveness of the vote counting rule to i assures us it may be), the ultimate outcome would have been x. So the voter confronts something of a strategic dilemma. This dilemma would be avoided, however, if both outcomes reachable from v_1 were no worse (or no better) than x. We previously identified voters with and without straightforward strategies in this example by examining the game form in Figure 11(d). Now we can see that we can make the same identification much more readily by direct examination of the reachable sets displayed in Figure 11(b). The voters who have straightforward strategies are precisely those whose preference orderings are 'separated' into the sets $\Gamma(v_0) = \{x\}$ and $\Gamma(v_1) = \{y, z\}$ as follows:

Separated				Non-separated	
R^1	R^2	R^4	R^6	R^3	R^5
x	x	y	z	y	z
y	z	z	y	x	x
z	y	x	x	z	y

More formally, and somewhat more broadly, we say (following Farquharson, 1956a and 1969a) that voter i's preference ordering is *weakly separated*

---

abstain.) If in addition the rule is (positively) responsive to 1, it follows that category (3) is *never* empty, so (-1) is the *unique* best reply in every contingency in the event $x P_i y$ and ($+1$) is the unique best reply in every contingency in the event $y P_i x$. (These propositions generalize to non-resolute vote counting rules if we assume that all voters rank the tie outcome between the two non-tie outcomes.)

by an agenda at decision node v if and only if, for all x in $\Gamma(v_0)$ and y in $\Gamma(v_1)$ either (i) $x R_i y$ or (ii) $y R_i x$. Voter i has a straightforward choice at a decision node if and only if his preference ordering is weakly separated at that node, and that choice is -1 if (i) is true and is $+1$ if (ii) is true. Suppose (i) is true; then it is certainly true that $x R_i y$ for all x in $C_i[\Gamma'(v_0)]$ and all y in $C_i[\Gamma'(v_1)]$; and likewise if (ii) is true. Thus a straightforward choice must be sincere. Considering the entire agenda tree, we now have *Farquharson's Straightforwardness Theorem: under any (non-repetitive) sequential binary procedure with a resolute and non-negatively responsive vote counting rule at each decision node, a voter has a straightforward voting strategy if and only if the agenda tree weakly separates his preference ordering at every decision node; moreover, this straightforward strategy, if it exists, is a sincere strategy.*

The agenda depicted in Figure 11 gives straightforward strategies to voters with 4 of the 6 possible strong preference orderings, and it may thereby suggest that voters commonly have straightforward strategies. However, this example is atypical, in that a small partition agenda is employed. Straightforwardness is less common under larger or non-partition agendas. In fact, no pairwise agenda on four or more alternatives can give any voter with strong preferences a straightforward strategy.[25]

Nevertheless, it may seem to be a desirable property of a voting procedure that no voter should ever have reason to regret voting sincerely, for otherwise 'an election [is] more of a game of skill than a real test of the wishes of the electors, and ... it is better for elections to be decided according to the wish of the majority than of those who happen to have the most skill at the game.'[26] So the question arises of whether it is possible to design a *strategyproof* voting procedure — that is, a voting procedure such that sincere voting is always straightforward. Recall that any non-negatively responsive and resolute vote counting rule is a strategyproof procedure for choosing between two alternatives. But we can readily see that no sequential binary procedure can be strategyproof given an agenda of three or more alternatives. If v is the initial node and $\Gamma(v)$ contains three or more alternatives, it follows that either $\Gamma(v_0)$ or $\Gamma(v_1)$ must contain at least two alternatives, one of which

---

[25] If $\Gamma(v)$ has four or more elements and the agenda is pairwise, at least two alternatives go unchallenged at the initial node v, so $\Gamma(v_0)$ and $\Gamma(v_1)$ can weakly separate a voter's preferences only if he is indifferent among those unchallenged alternatives.

[26] These words, often quoted, are from C. L. Dodgson's 'A Method of Taking Votes on More Than Two Issues'; see Black (1958: pp. 232–233).

may be the strictly most preferred, and the other the strictly least preferred, alternative of some voter i, in which case i's preference ordering cannot be weakly separated at v, so i cannot have a straightforward strategy.[27]

4.5. Sophisticated Voting Behavior

We have just seen that no sequential binary agenda with three or more alternatives can be strategyproof. Given an agenda of any magnitude, most voters most of the time do not have straightforward strategies. Given a pairwise agenda with four or more alternatives, no voter with strong preferences can have a straightforward strategy. Thus, it is inevitable that many voters much of the time may regret using their sincere voting strategies. How then should they vote?

As was noted in 4.3, some early works in voting and social choice theory treated this problem in an *ad hoc* way, but it remained for Robin Farquharson to address it in a systematic fashion. Farquharson's *Theory of Voting*[28] (1969a) provided a definition of 'sophisticated' voting and stated a theorem that says this: *if all voters have strong preferences, sophisticated voting under any sequential binary procedure leads to a determinate voting outcome.*

For a number of years, Farquharson's theory was applied hardly at all. Two considerations help explain why. First, his basic result is an 'existence' theorem; it tells us that something exists but not how to find it or what it looks like. Except for specific examples, Farquharson had little to say about the nature and consequences of sophisticated voting. Second, while Farquharson did present (1969a: pp. 64–67) a complete tabulation of sophisticated (as well as sincere) voting outcomes for the case of three voters and three alternatives under several procedures, and while he remarked in his Preface (1969a: p. xii) that this tabulation 'can readily be extended to cover any desired number of either,' the manner in which this extension can 'readily' be accomplished is not clear from his text. What is clear, as we shall

---

[27] A fundamental result due to Gibbard (1973) shows that, given three or more alternatives, no voting procedure whatsoever can be strategyproof.

[28] This work was actually written in the 1950s as a dissertation and parts of it were published at that time (1956a, 1956b); also see Dummett and Farquharson (1961). Unfortunately, publication of the complete work was delayed by more than a decade (also see Farquharson, 1966; 1969b), and Farquharson died shortly thereafter. It is an exceptionally clear and elegant work but is marred by a number of errors; for a useful compendium of corrections, see Niemi (1983).

see, is that the method that Farquharson overtly employed for identifying sophisticated voting strategies and outcomes is prohibitively burdensome given voting games of any greater magnitude. Fortunately, an alternate and much simpler method for identifying sophisticated voting strategies and outcomes has been developed.

We will introduce Farquharson's mode of analysis, and then the alternate method, by means of examples. Recall once again the successive agenda example displayed in Figure 11, and consider the specific voting game that results when the three voters have the following preference orderings.

EXAMPLE 4

Preference Profile   Majority Preference Tournament

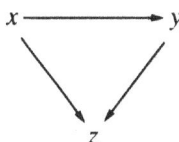

We previously saw that voter 1 has a straightforward strategy (s^1), but voters 2 and 3 do not. The consideration that dictates that voter 1 should use s^1 is this: in every contingency, s^1 gives at least as good an outcome as any other strategy; further, for each other strategy, there is some contingency in which s^1 gives a strictly better outcome. In game theory, it is commonly said that s^1 *dominates* every other strategy; Farquharson says that s^1 renders each other strategy *inadmissible*. Strategies not rendered inadmissible remain *admissible*. Given non-negative responsiveness in vote counting, a sincere voting strategy is always admissible, but other strategies may be admissible as well. However, not all other strategies are admissible.

In this respect, we should look more closely at the strategies available to voters 2 and 3. Consider voter 2 first. Relative to 2's preference ordering, s^1 dominates s^2 and s^3 dominates s^4. The logic that demands that voter 1 should not use any strategy other than s^1 also demands that voter 2 should not use any strategy other than s^1 or s^3, his two admissible strategies. Similar analysis reveals that voter 3 has just two admissible strategies, namely s^2 and s^4. As analysts, we have been able to identify the admissible strategies of each voter. If voters are strategically rational, voters can in like manner identify their own admissible strategies and will restrict their strategy selections accordingly. And, *if they know each other's preferences*, voters can also identify each other's admissible strategies and, *if they are confident of each other's rationality*, voters expect each other to select only admissible strategies. In this event, in selecting one of his (possibly) several admissible strategies, each voter need take account only of those contingencies made up of admissible strategies for other voters. Hence, considering admissible strategies only, we have the following (much) *reduced* game matrix (voter 1, with only one admissible strategy, has disappeared).

	s_3^2	s_3^4
s_2^1	x	x
s_2^3	x	y

Within this reduced game, s_2^3 *dominates* s_2^1 *(since* $y P_2 x$*) and* s_3^2 *dominate* s_3^4 *(since* $x P_3 y$*). Thus each of* voters 2 and 3 is left with a unique *secondarily admissible* voting strategy, while voter 1 has a unique (initially) admissible strategy. This triple of *ultimately admissible* strategies is the *sophisticated voting situation* (necessarily an individual voting equilibrium), which gives x as the *sophisticated voting outcome*.

Farquharson's Determinacy Theorem (1969a) says that *such a reduction to a unique sophisticated outcome always occurs if voters have strong preferences and if a resolute non-negatively responsive vote counting rule is used at every node of a sequential binary agenda.* However, the following elaboration is required. The reduction may have to proceed through several steps, to identify not only initially and secondarily inadmissible strategies but also *tertiarily inadmissible strategies*, and so forth. A strategy s_i is *ultimately admissible* if no further reduction is possible. Farquharson defines a *sophisticated voting strategy* as an ultimately admissible one. We shall call such a strategy *R-sophisticated* (for 'reduction-sophisticated'). His determinacy theorem states that all *R*-sophisticated voting situations give the same outcome, which is the *R*-sophisticated voting outcome.

There are several problems with all this. First, Farquharson's proof of the theorem is sketchy and incomplete — indeed, it really does not refer to sophisticated voting as he has defined it. Second, as noted earlier, the theorem is little more than an existence theorem. Third, the method Farquharson uses in his examples (and we used above) to identify sophisticated voting strategies is cumbersome even in three-voter, three-alternative cases. Farquharson constructs three-dimensional matrices (in the manner of Figure 11(c)) and reduces them according to the admissibility criteria. This method may be manageable for small scale examples (but even so there are number of errors in Farquharson's examples; see Niemi, 1983). But in voting games of any greater magnitude, this approach is wholly infeasible. In fact, we earlier (in 4.3) declined to construct the game form for even the three-voter three-alternative case under a standard amendment agenda, on the grounds it would have $8^3 = 512$ cells. The size of a game form explodes as voters or alternatives are added. Apart from anything else, this suggests that real-life voters would find it impossible to vote in a sophisticated fashion.

Fortunately, an alternate method for analyzing sophisticated voting (in conjunction with a slightly different definition of a sophisticated voting strategy) has been developed, which makes the identification of sophisticated voting strategies and outcomes extremely simple. This both permits us to prove a number of general propositions concerning sophisticated voting outcomes and also makes much more plausible the assumption that voters might actually use sophisticated voting strategies. This alternate method has been definitively characterized by McKelvey and Niemi (1978), who call it *multistage* sophisticated voting, because it exploits the multistage structure of voting under sequential binary procedure.

Let us once again consider the voting game specified by Figure 11 and Example 4. We saw before that strategies s^2 and s^4 were inadmissible for voter 2 and strategies s^1 and s^3 were inadmissible for voter 3. Why they are inadmissible becomes clear once we recall the specific choices entailed by these strategies and the structure of the agenda. Strategies s^2 and s^4 both require a voter at the final decision node v_1 to vote $+1$ (i.e., for y), rather than -1 (i.e., for z); such a choice is insincere for voter 2, who prefers y to z. Strategies s^1 and s^3 both require a voter at the final decision node v_1 to vote -1, rather than $+1$; such a choice is insincere for voter 3, who prefers z to y. We have seen that, within each subgame generated by the vote counting rule at any decision node, a voter has a straightforward choice if he has 'straightforward' preferences between the two outcomes. At the *final decision node*, these outcomes are simply alternatives so, *given nonnegative responsiveness of vote counting*, there is no reason for any voter to vote other than sincerely.

But if this is true *and if voters know each other's preferences* (or at least the collective preference yPz), at the initial decision node v, each voter can anticipate that the final outcome will be y if the voting process reaches node v_1. Thus, the choice at the initial node is *effectively* between x and y, not between x and $\{y, z\}$. Given non-negative responsiveness, all voters should choose sincerely between x (the actual outcome associated with outcome node v_0) and y (the anticipated outcome associated with decision node v_1). Therefore, at the initial decision node, voters 1 and 3 should vote -1 (i.e., for x), and 2 should vote $+1$ (i.e., for an anticipated y), and x is the voting outcome if everyone votes in a 'sophisticated' fashion.

This *backwards induction* logic can be generalized and formalized. Following McKelvey and Niemi (1978), we associate with each node v of the agenda tree an alternative $s(v)$ called the *sophisticated equivalent*, defined as follows:

(1) if $\Gamma(v)$ is a one-element set $\{x\}$ (i.e., if v is an outcome node), $s(v) = x$; and
(2) otherwise (i.e., if v is a decision node)
    (a) if $s(v_0)\ P\ s(v_1)$, $s(v) = s(v_0)$,
    (b) if $s(v_1)\ P\ s(v_0)$, $s(v) = s(v_1)$, and
    (c) if $s(v_0) = s(v_1)$, $s(v) = s(v_0) = s(v_1)$.

(The collective preference P is that entailed by voter preferences in conjunction with the particular vote counting rule employed at node v.) A voter i's *sophisticated choice* at node v is -1 if $s(v_0)\ P_i\ s(v_1)$, is $+1$ if $s(v_1)\ P_i s(v_0)$, and is either -1 or $+1$ if $s(v_0) = s(v_1)$. A voter's *sophisticated voting strategy* is one made up of sophisticated choices at every node. We call such a strategy *MS-sophisticated* (for 'multistage sophisticated'). Though voters may have several such sophisticated strategies, all *MS*-sophisticated voting situations give the same *MS*-sophisticated voting outcome if all voters have strong preferences. Moreover, this sophisticated outcome can be readily identified (without first identifying sophisticated strategies): *under any sequential binary procedure, the MS-sophisticated outcome is simply the sophisticated equivalent at the initial decision node.*[29]

---

[29]This backwards induction argument in fact was not new to McKelvey and Niemi's work. It is in effect the argument that Farquharson used to support his determinacy theorem, even though he defined sophisticated voting differently and argument is not correct given that definition. Backwards induction had been used in some earlier works, several of which apparently accepted

What is the relationship between R-sophisticated and MS-sophisticated strategies and outcomes? In any particular voting game, the set of R-sophisticated and MS-sophisticated strategies may fail to coincide; thus the reduction and multistage definitions of sophistication are logically distinct. However, as McKelvey and Niemi conjectured and Gretlein (1983) subsequently demonstrated, the sophisticated voting *outcome* is the same under either definition. Accordingly, we may henceforth speak generically of *sophisticated voting outcomes*.[30]

4.6. Cooperative Voting Behavior

To this point, we have assumed that all voters select their voting strategies — be they sincere or sophisticated — in isolation from one another. Suppose, on the other hand, that voters can enter into *coalitions* — that is, make agreements to coordinate their voting strategies.

Let us consider the voting game form in Figure 11 in conjunction with the following (cyclical) preference profile.

$$
\begin{array}{ccc}
\underline{1} & \underline{2} & \underline{3} \\
z & y & x \\
x & z & y \\
y & x & z
\end{array}
$$

Following the earlier labelling of strategies, s^3 is straightforward for voter 2 and s^1 is straightforward for voter 3. Let us hold voter 3's strategy choice constant at s^1 and focus on the first four columns of the game form in Figure 11(d) to examine strategic interactions between voters 1 and 2.

The sincere voting situation (s_1^4, s_2^3, s_3^1) is vulnerable to voter 1, as (s_1^2, s_2^3, s_3^1) gives x as the outcome, which 1 prefers to y. Since both other voters are using straightforward strategies, this is the sophisticated voting

---

Farquharson's definition and others of which made no reference to him. For a related analysis, see Moulin (1979).

[30]While we ordinarily assume simple majority rule at every decision node, this is not required for outcomes to be anticipated and sophisticated strategies to be identified. Sincere voting behavior is not affected by vote counting rules, though the rules affect the outcome resulting from such behavior. Sophisticated behavior, on the other hand, is affected by vote counting rules (because such rules affect collective preference and thus sophisticated equivalents), but it can be analyzed with equal facility whatever the rules.

situation and is an individual equilibrium. But while this situation is vulnerable to no *individual* voter, it *is* vulnerable to a *coalition* of voters in that, if
1 and 2 *jointly* switch to s^4, the resulting situation gives z as the outcome,
which 1 and 2 *both* prefer to x. Following Farquharson (1969a), we say a
situation s giving alternative x is *vulnerable to coalition C* of voters if there
is a another situation s', differing from s only with respect to the strategies of
voters in C, such that s' gives alternative y and all voters in C prefer y to x.
A situation is a *collective equilibrium* if it is not vulnerable to *any* coalition
of voters.

We have observed that (s_1^2, s_2^3, s_3^1) fails to be a collective equilibrium,
because it is vulnerable to the coalition of 1 and 2. Yet even if voters 1 and 2
can communicate and agree to coordinate on s_4, we cannot be sure that this
agreement will be implemented, because the resulting situation (s_1^4, s_2^4, s_3^1)
itself fails to be a collective equilibrium. And it fails to be so in two distinct
ways.

First, (s_1^4, s_2^4, s_3^1) is itself vulnerable to a *subset of the coalition* that agreed
to it; voter 2 has an incentive to defect from the agreement by switching back
to his (straightforward) strategy s^3. In this sense, the coalition agreement
is *internally vulnerable*. The reason for this vulnerability becomes clear if
we look back to the sequential structure of the agenda depicted in Figure
11(a) and 11(b). Voter 1's sincere choice at initial node v is $+1$, but voter
1 can anticipate that, if v_1 is reached, the ultimate outcome will be y, his
least preferred alternative. Therefore, the effective choice at the initial node
is between x and $y = s(v_1)$, so 1's sophisticated choice at the initial node
is -1, resulting in x as the outcome. Voters 1 and 2, however, have a
common interest in bringing about z as the outcome, rather than x, and
they can realize this common interest by agreeing to the following: voter 1
promises to choose (contrary to his sophisticated strategy) $+1$ at the *initial*
node v and, in exchange, voter 2 promises to choose (contrary to his sincere,
sophisticated, and straightforward strategy) $+1$ at the *second* node v_1. The
difficulty is now clear: once voter 1 has kept his promise at the first node,
voter 2 has every incentive to *renege* on his promise at the second node
and thereby make his most preferred alternative y the outcome. Voter 2
may well be unable to persuade 1 that he will *not* renege, in which case the
bargain cannot be consummated or, if it is, 2 may indeed renege — unless
1, anticipating 2's perfidy, reneges first. Despite such considerations, the
theory of cooperative voting (following cooperative game theory generally)
assumes that voters can somehow make *binding commitments*, so that the

problem of internally vulnerable coalition agreements is overcome.[31] Thus, given cooperative voting, voter 2 can commit himself to vote for z (his second preference) rather than y (his first preference), and is thereby empowered to enter into a mutually beneficial coalition with voter 1.

Second, $\left(s_1^4, s_2^4, s_3^1\right)$ fails to be a collective equilibrium, not only because it is vulnerable to a subset of the original coalition, but also because it is vulnerable to another quite different (though overlapping) coalition. In this sense, the coalition agreement is *externally vulnerable* — voters outside the coalition C that might make the agreement can profitably preempt the agreement by offering a different agreement giving an outcome some members of C prefer. In the present example, the potential agreement between voters 1 and 2 creates the prospect of total defeat for voter 3, in that it gives his least preferred alternative z as the outcome. Moreover, 3 can offer 2 better terms: coordination on strategy s^3, which gives y (which both prefer to z) as the outcome. But the situation $\left(s_1^4, s_2^3, s_3^3\right)$ that would result from this agreement is likewise externally vulnerable, in this case to the coalition of 1 and 3, who can coordinate their strategies so as the bring about z as the outcome. And in like manner, we can follow around the cycle in majority preference indefinitely.

Cooperative voting outcomes thus depend on the pattern of external vulnerability (or invulnerability) of coalition agreements. If the vote counting rule at every decision node is majority rule, external vulnerability depends entirely on (absolute) majority preference; if an odd number of voters have strong preferences, such vulnerability depends on the majority preference tournament — that is, an agreement giving x as the outcome is externally vulnerable if and only if there is some y such that $y P x$.[32]

In considering cooperative voting, we may suppose that, before any voting occurs, negotiations take place among voters. If we assume away problems of internal vulnerability, this bargaining process is driven entirely by the pattern of external vulnerability and thus, if the vote counting rule

---

[31] Two rationales are commonly offered for supposing that internally vulnerable agreements will be made and carried out. One is that players can make 'contracts' that are reliably enforced by some outside authority (e.g., courts). The other, more plausible in the context of voting, is that players are concerned to acquire a reputation for trustworthiness that will enable them to make beneficial agreements in the future. The analysis in this section is especially pertinent to 'logrolling agreements'; see footnote 20 and citations therein.

[32] On the other hand, if a two-thirds vote (for example) is required for final passage, external vulnerability is more complex, with the result that several distinct agreements (giving different outcomes) may all be externally invulnerable.

is everywhere majority rule, by majority preference. Cooperative voting outcomes are, accordingly, entirely independent of the agenda structure, i.e., the order in which alternatives are voted on and the particular procedure in use.[33] The resulting coalition agreement is then implemented through the voting process, as members of the supporting coalition vote in the agreed upon fashion (probably by voting as a bloc at every node) to carry the voting path from the initial node to an outcome node giving the negotiated alternative.

5. SOLUTION SETS

We now consider how to define 'best' or 'collectively most preferred' alternatives. This has significance from the perspective of social choice theory and the normative questions identified in the introductory section, but our primary motivation concerns the relevance of such analysis for the descriptive analysis of committee voting outcomes. From the perspective of descriptive theory, the term *solution set* commonly refers to a set of alternatives that includes all possible outcomes of a voting process, given certain behavioral assumptions. In the following discussion, majority preference is taken to be the relevant collective preference relation.

5.1. Unbeaten Alternatives and the Condorcet Winner

A 'best' alternative might be defined as an alternative that is most preferred by all members of a coalition of some requisite (e.g., majority) size. We call an alternative x a *majority winner* in X if a majority of voters most prefer x among all alternatives in X. Given an odd number of voters with strong preferences, a majority winner is assured if $|X| = 2$, but otherwise first preferences may be so dispersed that no majority winner exists.

Condorcet proposed a somewhat weaker definition of a 'best' alternative — x is a *Condorcet winner* in X if x beats every other alternative in X. A majority winner beats every other alternative *through the same majority coalition*; a Condorcet winner beats every other alternative but (in general) *beats different alternatives through different majority coalitions*. Thus, a

---

[33] More generally, the ability of voters to make binding agreements and commitments neutralizes the sequential structure of committee voting; for related discussions, see Shepsle and Weingast (1984b) and Ingberman and Yao (1991).

majority winner is necessarily a Condorcet winner but the reverse is not true. The following provides an example.

EXAMPLE 5

	Preference Profile 1			Preference Profile 2		Majority Preference Tournament
1	2	3	1	2	3	
x	x	y	y	x	z	
y	z	z	x	y	x	
z	y	x	z	z	y	

In Preference Profile 1, x is the majority (and Condorcet) winner; in Profile 2, x is the Condorcet (but not majority) winner. This example also illustrates related points. First, even apart from the identity of a fixed number of voters, distinct preference profiles may underlie the same majority preference tournament. Second, whether a Condorcet winner is a majority winner depends on the underlying preference profile and cannot be determined on the basis of the majority preference tournament itself.

If majority preference is weak, the notion of a (single) Condorcet winner generalizes to the set of *unbeaten alternatives* (which set, in game theory, is called the *core*). We also introduce a related definition: a *Condorcet loser* in X is an alternative that is beaten by every other alternative in X.

Though a Condorcet winner may exist when a majority winner does not, cyclical majority preference means that there may be no Condorcet winner (or unbeaten alternative), as Example 1 illustrates. Since different restrictions on preferences have different consequences for the transitivity of majority preference (as discussed in 3.6), they also have different consequences for the existence of unbeaten alternatives and a Condorcet winner.

Single peakedness precludes majority preference cycles and therefore assures that there is an unbeaten alternative and, if n is odd, a Condorcet winner, which can be readily identified by the 'median voter theorem' originally due to Black (1948). If voter preferences are single-peaked, there is a strong ordering S of alternatives, which in turn induces a weak ordering on voters in terms of their most preferred alternatives or ideal points. If the number of voters n is odd, with respect to this ordering there is a unique *median alternative* (or ideal point) x^{med} (perhaps shared by several voters), such that no more than $n/2$ of the voters have most preferred alternatives on either side of x^{med}. *Black's* (1948, 1958) *Median Voter Theorem* states that, in the case of odd n, x^{med} *beats every alternative to its left* (being preferred by the median voter and every voter to his right, by definition constituting a majority) *and every point to its right* (by similar reasoning) *and is therefore the Condorcet winner.*[34]

When we turn to the multidimensional case with standard spatial preferences, there is no assurance that unbeaten points exist. In fact, the conditions for the existence of an unbeaten point are extremely restrictive. To illustrate this, let us consider the case of a two-dimensional space with an odd number of voters with Euclidean preferences.[35] Any line L through the alternative space partitions the ideal points into three sets: those that lie on one side of L, those that lie on the other side of L, and those that lie on L. A *median line M* partitions the ideal points so that no more than half of them lie on either side M. Any median line M is externally stable (as defined in 3.6, i.e., for any point z not on M, we can find some point on M that beats z). To see this, we draw a line L through z perpendicular to M. Then, applying the median voter theorem to the (single-peaked) induced voter preferences on the line L, it follows that the point at the intersection of L and M is the median induced ideal point on L and beats every other point on L, including z. Thus no unbeaten point can lie off of any median line, which means such a point exists if and only if *all* median lines (typically infinite in number) intersect at a common point. While it is true that median lines typically pass near the center of the distribution of ideal points in the space, the likelihood of their intersecting at a single point is essentially zero. Thus there is almost never an unbeaten point; if perchance there is such a point, it is unique, a Condorcet winner, and the ideal point of some voter.

With multiple issues and separable preferences, it follows from the discussion in 3.6 that there is a Condorcet winner among the alternatives only if there is a 'Condorcet position' on *every* issue; further Example 2 demonstrates that this condition is not sufficient. If all issues are

---

[34] Given an alternative continuum and an even number of voters, there may be two distinct median voter ideal points $x^{med'}$ and $x^{med''}$ that are unbeaten, a property also shared by all points on the interval between $x^{med'}$ and $x^{med''}$.

[35] This argument, and also the definition of the 'yolk' given in 5.2, generalizes straightforwardly to any number of dimensions if we replace references to 'lines' by references to 'hyperplanes.' The following exposition is drawn from Miller, Grofman, and Feld (1989).

dichotomous, either the alternative made up of majority positions on all issues is the Condorcet winner or there is no such alternative.

Given individualistic preferences over pure allocations, it follows from the discussion in 3.6 that a Condorcet winner cannot exist. Given a distributive context, the only possible Condorcet winner is the *null* project package <0,...,0>, and it is only if projects are highly inefficient.

5.2. The Top Cycle Set

Unbeaten alternative may not exist, yet it seems that some alternatives may still be 'better' than others. Certainly, voting produces outcomes in any event. Thus we have reason to identify solution sets guaranteed to be non-empty.

Consider Figure 12, which displays a majority preference tournament with eight alternatives. (To make the diagram more readable, single arrows replace certain collections of arrows all pointing in the same direction.) Note that there is no Condorcet winner. Nevertheless, it may be appropriate to identify the set $\{x_1, \dots, x_4\}$ as 'best,' since each alternative in this set beats every alternative outside it. The same is true of $\{x_1, \dots, x_5\}$ but $\{x_1, \dots, x_4\}$ is the *smallest* set with this property. This suggests the following definition. If collective preference is strong and represented by a tournament, the *top cycle set* $TC(X)$ of alternatives in X is the non-empty set such that: (1) for every pair of alternatives x in $TC(X)$ and y not in $TC(X)$, xPy; and (2) no proper subset of $TC(X)$ meets condition (1). Since the whole set X meets condition (1), a top cycle set always exists. Furthermore, if there is a Condorcet winner x^*, $\{x^*\} = TC(X)$. Given any tournament on X, the following points also hold (Miller, 1977b): (1) there is a unique set $TC(X)$; (2) in the absence of a Condorcet winner, $TC(X)$ contains at least three alternatives and there is a complete cycle of majority preference in $TC(X)$ (hence the name 'top cycle'); (3) for every alternative x in $TC(X)$, there is a complete path in X beginning with x; and (4) $\bar{P}(x) = X$ if and only if x belongs to $TC(X)$.[36]

---

[36] If majority preference is weak, a distinction arises between (i) a minimal set of alternatives X' such that xRy for all x in X' and y not in X' and (ii) a minimal set of alternatives X'' such that xPy for all x in X'' and y not in X''. Such sets always exist. There may be several (disjoint) sets of the former type but there can be only one of the latter, and the union of the former is a subset of the latter. In social choice theory, the union of the former has been dubbed the GOTCHA set and the latter the GETCHA set by Schwartz (1986).

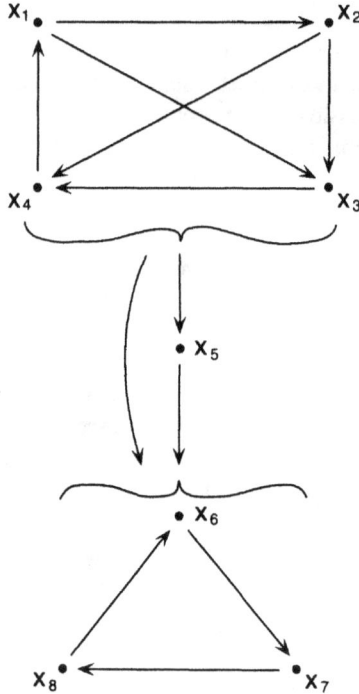

FIGURE 12 A top cycle set

Given standard spatial preferences in two or more dimensions, we have seen that a Condorcet winner almost never exists. But this result seems to leave open the possibility that the top cycle set may be a small subset of the space. However, *McKelvey's* (1976, 1979) *Global Cycling Theorem* tells us this: *if there is no Condorcet winner, a global top cycle encompasses the entire alternative space.*

McKelvey demonstrated this initially (1976) for the case of Euclidean preferences. We can explicate this result by using an analytical device that will also be useful later. We saw earlier that an unbeaten point exists only if all median lines intersect at a single point, which is extremely unlikely. But it does seem likely that typically all median lines pass near the center of the distribution of ideal points, so that there is a fairly small region through which all median lines pass. Following McKelvey (1986) and others (Ferejohn, McKelvey, and Packel, 1984; Miller, Grofman, and Feld, 1989), we define the *yolk* as the region bounded by the circle of minimum radius that intersects every median line. The location of the yolk is specified by its *center c* and its size by its *radius r*. The location of the yolk indicates the generalized center of the distribution of ideal points. The size of the yolk indicates the extent to which the configuration of ideal points departs from one that generates an unbeaten point.

Using the yolk construction, we can show two things (Miller, Grofman, and Feld, 1989): (1) if point z is more than $2r$ further from the center of the yolk c than x is, x beats z; and (2), provided r is greater than zero, for any point x there is some other point z that both beats x and is (not more than $2r$) further from the center of the yolk than x is. Given these two facts, it follows that we can always construct a cycle that includes any two points in the space and therefore that the top cycle can never be confined to an area smaller than the whole space.[37] A corollary of the first point is that, if there is a Condorcet winner (so $r = 0$), $P(x)$ for any x is the area enclosed by the circle centered on c and passing through x.

Turning to separable preferences over multiple issues, we have already seen that intransitivies over individual issue positions are inherited by alternatives composed of packages of issue positions. This implies that $TC(X)$, where X is the Cartesian product of issues $X^1 \times \cdots \times X^k$, is at least as encompassing as the Cartesian product $TC(X^1) \times \cdots \times TC(X^k)$. But $TC(X)$ may be far more encompassing and may include the entire set of alternatives even where $TC(X^1) \times \cdots \times TC(X^k)$ is a one-element set, i.e., where every issue has a Condorcet position (as is necessarily true if all issues are dichotomous). This is illustrated both by Example 2 and by the multidimensional spatial case with Euclidean or otherwise separable preferences, where each dimension is taken to be an issue.

Consideration of the scope of the top cycle set among allocative alternatives is of historical interest, because it was in this context that the top cycle concept was first formulated by Ward (1961), who determined that the top cycle set includes essentially every alternative. In a distributive context, if and only if the null package fails to be a Condorcet winner, every

---

[37] In his later paper (1979), McKelvey proved a similar result for a much broader class of voter preferences.

pair of packages is mutually reachable and $TC(X)$ encompasses all possible alternatives (Miller, 1982; also see Shepsle and Weingast, 1981; Fiorina, 1981).

5.3. The Uncovered Set

We should note one particular way in which the top cycle set appears to be excessively inclusive. $TC(X)$ is not, in general, a subset of the set of Pareto-optimal alternatives $PO(X)$. We have noted this implicitly in the case of particularistic preferences, by observing that the top cycle includes essentially all alternatives (including inefficient ones). We have also noted this implicitly in the multidimensional spatial case, by demonstrating global cycles while the Pareto-optimal set is clearly bounded.[38] The example below provides a specific example of this phenomenon, as $PO(X) = \{x, y, z\}$ while $TC(X) = \{x, y, z, v\}$.

EXAMPLE 6

Preference Profile   Majority Preference Tournament

1	2	3
x	y	z
y	z	v
z	v	x
v	x	y

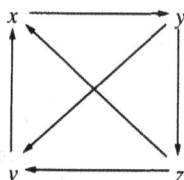

Despite these problems, until the mid-to-late 1970s, it appeared that the top cycle set was the smallest solution that could be defined. Encompassing cycles within the top cycle set suggested that it could not be 'split open' in any meaningful way. More recent research has indicated that this view was mistaken and that majority preference has deeper structure which allows for the definition of less inclusive solution sets which have a bearing on voting theory.

One step in this direction is provided by the *covering relation*, first explicitly proposed by Miller (1980). Suppose majority preference over

---

[38]Given Euclidean preferences, $PO(X)$ is the *convex hull* of voter ideal points, i.e., the minimal convex set including all voter ideal points.

a fixed set X of alternatives is strong and represented by a tournament. Then we say x *covers* y, written xCy, if $P(x)$ is a subset of $P(y)$. In words, x covers y if everything in X that beats x also beats y. Given a tournament structure, this implies that x beats everything that y beats and also that x beats y. The covering relation C is incomplete but transitive, and it subsumes the Pareto relation.

For a fixed X, let $UC(x)$ be the set of alternatives *not* covered by x (note that x belongs to $UC(x)$), and let the *uncovered set* $UC(X)$ be the set of alternatives not covered by any other alternative in X. Given a majority preference tournament, the following points hold (Miller, 1980 and 1983; Banks, 1985): (1) $UC(X)$ is never empty; (2) if there is a Condorcet winner x^*, $UC(X) = \{x^*\}$; (3) otherwise, $UC(X)$ includes at least three alternatives; (4) $UC(X)$ is a subset of both $TC(X)$ and $PO(X)$; (5) for every y not in $UC(X)$, there is some x in $UC(X)$ such that xCy; and (6) every alternative in X is reachable from any alternative in $UC(X)$ by a path of no more than two steps (the *two-step principle*). Finally, if the uncovered set has just three elements or if it is identical to the top cycle set, it contains a complete cycle; otherwise, if we consider only the subtournament comprised of the alternatives in $UC(X)$ and the arrows among them, we may find that it has its own top cycle, so that $TC[UC(X)]$ is a proper subset of $UC(X)$ (but always with at least three elements). In Figure 12, x_2Cx_3, so $UC(X) = \{x_1, x_2, x_4\}$.[39]

Miller (1980) originally conjectured that, in the spatial case, the uncovered set would be a relatively small subset of the Pareto-optimal set, centrally located in the distribution of ideal points, and that it would shrink in size as the number and diversity of ideal points increase. Though work remains to be done in this area, these conjectures have been generally borne out. In the case of Euclidean preferences, it is possible to put a bound on the location and size of the uncovered set. Recall the result that a point x beats any other point y that is more than $2r$ (where r is the radius of the yolk) further from the center c of the yolk than x is. Likewise any such y beats any z that is more than $2r$ further from the center of the yolk than y is or $4r$ further from the center of the yolk than x is. Thus, x covers any point z that is more than $4r$ further from the center of the yolk than x is. As a corollary,

---

[39] In the event majority preference is weak, there is no unique generalization of the covering relation as defined for tournaments. A variety of definitions may be found in the literature; under all such definitions, Pareto optimality and some variant of the two-step principle still hold. (For a partial summary, see Bordes, 1983.) Given standard spatial preferences, the differences in definitions affect only whether the uncovered set contains its own boundary.

$UC(c)$ is contained within the ball centered on c with radius of $4r$. Since the uncovered set is comprised of those points not covered by *any* other point, $UC(X)$ is contained within $UC(c)$ and within the same ball of $4r$ radius.[40]

On the other hand, given particularistic preferences, the uncovered set does not narrow down the set of efficient outcomes. In the case of pure allocation, the uncovered set includes essentially all efficient allocations (McKelvey, 1986; Epstein, 1992), and a comparable result holds in the distributive case (Miller, 1982).

5.4. The Banks Set

We discuss one additional solution set, due to Banks (1985). Given a majority preference tournament on X, consider the following construction. We pick an arbitrary alternative x_1 in the tournament; we next pick an alternative x_2 that beats x_1; we then pick a third alternative x_3 that beats both x_2 and x_1; and so forth. Proceeding in this manner, we construct a *chain* of alternatives, i.e., an ordered set $< x_k, x_{k-1}, \ldots, x_2, x_1 >$ such that $x_h P x_g$ if and only if $k \geq h > g \geq 1$. The *bottom* element of the chain is beaten by all other elements. Let $H(x)$ designate a chain with *top* element x that beats all other elements. Suppose we continue to assemble the chain until no new top element can be added. We call such an *externally stable* (as defined in 3.6) chain a *Banks chain*. Let $H^+(x)$ designate a Banks chain with top element x. The top element of a Banks chain is a *Banks alternative*. Let $B(X:z)$ designate the set of top elements of all chains in X with bottom element z. The *Banks set* $B(X)$ of alternatives consists, of all Banks alternatives. Clearly, if x covers y, y cannot be a Banks alternative.[41] Thus $B(X)$ is a subset of $UC(X)$ and in turn a subset of both $TC(X)$ and $PO(X)$. However, the Banks set is distinct from the uncovered set only if the latter is moderately large. Further, $B(X)$ must be contained within the top cycle of $UC(X)$ and,

---

[40] See McKelvey (1986) and Miller, Grofman, and Feld (1989). Apart from those cases in which a Condorcet winner exists, the only spatial case in which the uncovered set has been precisely demarcated is the simplest possible case of three voters with Euclidean preferences in two-dimensions (Feld, *et al.*, 1987; Hartley and Kilgour, 1987). Support for the general proposition that the size of the yolk decreases as the number and diversity of voter ideal points increase is provided by Feld, Grofman,and Miller (1987) and Tovey (1992).

[41] Suppose that y were the top element of some chain $H(y)$. On the one hand, x cannot be in $H(y)$ because $x P y$. So x must be outside $H(y)$. But x beats y and everything y beats and thus everything else in $H(y)$. So $H(y)$ is not externally stable and is not a Banks chain. Since the same argument can be made for any other chain $H'(y)$, y cannot be a Banks alternative.

in any event, the Banks set itself has a complete cycle. (For details, see Banks, 1985; Moulin, 1986; Miller, Grofman, and Feld, 1990b.)

6. VOTING OUTCOMES

We are now in a position to analyze voting outcomes under different agendas and behavioral assumptions. We assume that some *sequential binary procedure* is in use, that the vote counting rule at every decision node is *majority rule*, and that majority preference over the agenda set is a *tournament*.[42]

A definite voting outcome is entailed once we specify the following: (a) the agenda set A, (b) the voter preference profile over A, (c) the behavioral assumption pertaining to voters, and (d) the agenda structure. Commonly, we allow (d) — and the voting order in particular — to vary, and we ask which alternatives, defined with reference to their position in voter preferences, are possible voting outcomes. A natural question, for example is whether a Condorcet winner in A is the only possible voting outcome. We will also see the relevance of other solution sets for voting outcomes.

In general, we let $S(A)$ designate the set of possible voting outcomes from an agenda set A. We refine this designation to $SIN(A)$, $SOPH(A)$, and $COOP(A)$ according to the behavioral assumption (sincere, sophisticated, and cooperative voting respectively). We further refine this designation to the form $S|P(A)$ according to the type of agenda P in use. The category P is specified as follows: SB, all sequential binary agendas; S, successive (or sequential) agendas; UP, all uniform partition agendas; BB, bill-by-bill (or Plott–Levine) agendas; PW, all pairwise agendas; A, amendment agendas; and $A2$, two-stage amendment agendas.

Because many specific results are reported in the remaining sections, it is convenient to present them as explicit numbered propositions. The propositions in this section are of interest in themselves and also provide a foundation for those in the concluding sections on agenda control and formation.

---

[42] If ties can occur and are broken in the manner of the standard parliamentary vote counting rule (recall 1.2), the GETCHA set (see footnote 36) generally plays the role of $TC(A)$ in the various propositions.

6.1. Voting Outcome Algorithms

Sincere voting outcomes may always be determined by constructing the appropriate agenda tree and 'simulating' the sincere voting process: that is, given a preference profile, we may determine how each voter, and thus a majority of voters, would vote at the initial node of the agenda, then at the resulting node, and so forth. In this way, we may trace the *sincere voting path* through the agenda tree to its outcome node.

In parallel manner, sophisticated voting outcomes may always be determined by constructing the appropriate agenda tree and then identifying the sophisticated equivalent at each decision node, starting from final decision nodes and working back up the tree to the initial node. The sophisticated equivalent at the initial node is the sophisticated voting outcome. (If desired, we can also trace *sophisticated voting paths* through the agenda tree.)

However, two types of agendas — amendment (forward- or backward-built) and successive (or sequential) — exhibit an important kind of regularity in that, once the alternatives are placed in a *voting order*, the agenda structure is determined.[43] The regularity of such procedures makes it possible to devise algorithms for determining voting outcomes once the voting order is fixed. Especially in the case of sophisticated voting under amendment procedure, these algorithms are substantially more convenient than the general procedures identified above and lead to useful theoretical insights.[44] Formally, each algorithm involves construction of a (*sincere* or *sophisticated*) *equivalent agenda*, which is a list of m alternatives, one for each order of node 0 through $m - 1$ in the agenda, each of which represents a *potential outcome* d_h under sincere voting or an *anticipated outcome* z_h under sophisticated voting at that order of node.

A given alternative may appear in an equivalent agenda in several consecutive positions, from which it follows that other alternatives may never appear. Elements of A that never appear in an equivalent agenda are called *innocuous*.[45] The first alternative in the voting order always appears as the first element of a sincere equivalent agenda, and the last alternative in the

[43] Mostly for this reason, voting decisions under amendment and successive procedures have received the greatest, and often parallel, attention in voting theory; other works have focused exclusively on amendment procedure.

[44] The following terminology and analysis is adapted from Jung (1990), who in turn draws from Miller (1977b) and Shepsle and Weingast (1984a).

[45] This generalizes a term introduced by Shepsle and Weingast (1984a). Removal of an innocuous alternative from an agenda (the voting order among the remaining alternatives

voting order always appears as the last element of a sophisticated equivalent agenda, and each is therefore trivially non-innocuous. The last element of a sincere equivalent agenda, and the first element of a sophisticated equivalent agenda, is the voting outcome.

Given the significance of the voting order under these two procedures, in this section we subscript alternatives $x_1, x_2, \ldots, x_m$ to indicate their position from first to last in that voting order. We do not here single out the status quo for special attention or otherwise take account of the parliamentary status of alternatives, and there is no distinction between forward- and backward-built amendment agendas or between successive and sequential agendas.

Use of the voting outcome algorithms will be illustrated by the following example.

EXAMPLE 7

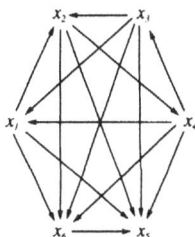

| Preference Profile | Majority Preference Tournament |

Given the voting order indicated by the subscripts, the successive and amendment agenda trees are shown in Figures 13(a) and (b). (To save space, outcome nodes are omitted from Figure 13(b).)

Sincere Voting Under Successive Procedure Under a successive (or sequential) agenda, the sincere voting outcome is the *first* alternative x_g in the voting order that is the *majority winner* in the set of alternatives not already rejected, i.e., in $\{x_g, x_{g+1}, \ldots, x_m\}$. Note that, in order to identify x_g and to implement the algorithm below, we must know the voter preference profile.

remaining as before) *always* leaves the voting outcome unchanged; likewise, the addition of an alternative to an agenda always leaves the voting outcome unchanged, if the added alternative is innocuous in the expanded agenda. (The same is *sometimes* true of non-innocuous alternatives.)

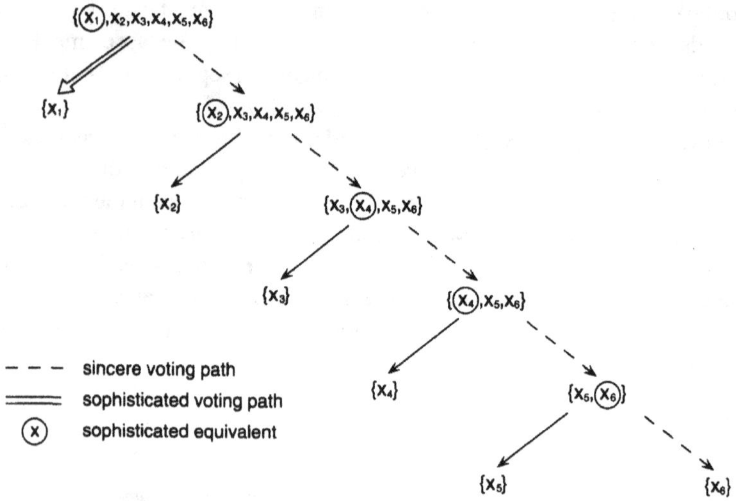

　　　　　　　　　NICHOLAS R. MILLER

FIGURE 13(a)　The Successive Agenda for Example 7

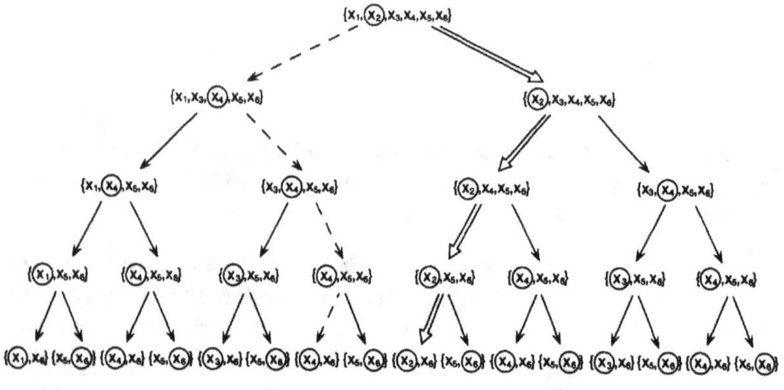

FIGURE 13(b)　The Amendment Agenda for Example 7

(In contrast, the remaining three algorithms depend only on the majority preference tournament.) Thus the *sincere equivalent agenda under successive procedure* is defined inductively as:

$$d_1 = x_1; \text{ and for all } 2 \leq h \leq m$$

$$d_h = \begin{cases} d_{h-1} \text{ if } |i \text{ such that } d_{h-1}P_i x_k \text{ for all } k \geq h| > n/2 \\ x_h \text{ otherwise.} \end{cases}$$

The sincere equivalent agenda under successive procedure for Example 7 is $(d_1, ..., d_6) = (x_1, x_2, x_3, x_4, x_5, x_6)$, reflecting that no alternative prior to x_6 is a majority winner in the set of alternatives not yet rejected. Thus x_6 is, the sincere outcome and no alternative is innocuous. Since a majority of voters have either x_5 or or x_6 as, their first preference (and x_6 beats x_5), the sincere voting path (shown in Figure 13(a)) follows right-branching path of maximum length leading to the outcome node giving x_6. For sincere voting under successive procedures an alternative is innocuous if and only if it follows the voting outcome in the voting order.

Sincere Voting Under Amendment Procedure Under amendment procedure, the sincere voting outcome is the *first* (and only) alternative x_g in the voting order that both (a) beats the alternative with which it is initially paired and (b) is the *Condorcet winner* in the set of alternatives not yet defeated, i.e., $\{x_g, x_{g+1}, \ldots, x_m\}$. Thus the *sincere equivalent agenda under amendment procedure* is defined inductively as:

$$d_1 = x_1; \text{ and for all } 2 \leq h \leq m$$

$$d_h = \begin{cases} d_{h-1} \text{ if } d_{h-1}Px_h \\ x_h \text{ if } x_h P d_{h-1}. \end{cases}$$

The sincere equivalent agenda under amendment procedure for Example 7 is $(d_1, ..., d_6) = (x_1, x_1, x_3, x_4, x_4, x_4)$, reflecting that x_1 beats x_2 but is beaten by x_3; x_3 then loses to x_4, which beats all remaining alternatives. Thus x_4 is the sincere outcome and x_2, x_5, and x_6 are innocuous. The sincere voting path is shown in Figure 13(b). For sincere voting under amendment procedure, an alternative is innocuous if and only if it is beaten by the potential outcome at the time it enters the voting; this implies that every alternative that follows the voting outcome in the voting order is innocuous.

Sophisticated Voting Under Successive Procedure The sophisticated equivalent at the final decision node v'' is the majority preferred alternative in the pair x_m and x_{m-1}; the sophisticated equivalent at the next-to-final decision node v' is the majority preferred alternative in the pair $s(v'')$ and x_{m-2}; and so forth. It follows that the sophisticated equivalent agenda under successive procedure is identical to the sincere equivalent agenda under amendment procedure *when the order of voting is reversed* (Miller, 1977b); we call this the *reversibility property*. Thus, under successive procedure, the sophisticated voting outcome is the *last* (and only) alternative x_g in the voting order that both (a) beats the sophisticated equivalent with which it is paired and (b) is the *Condorcet winner* in the set of alternatives not yet so paired, i.e., $\{x_1, \ldots, x_{g-1}, x_g\}$. Thus the *sophisticated equivalent agenda under successive procedure* is defined by backwards induction as:

$$z_m = x_m; \text{ and for all } m - 1 \geq h \geq 1$$

$$z_h = \begin{cases} z_{h+1} \text{ if } z_{h+1} P x_h \\ x_h \text{ if } x_h P z_{h+1}. \end{cases}$$

The sophisticated equivalent agenda under successive procedure for Example 7 is $(z_1, \ldots, z_6) = (x_1, x_2, x_4, x_4, x_6, x_6)$, reflecting that x_6 beats x_5 but loses to x_4; x_4 beats x_3 but loses to x_2, which in turn loses to x_1. Thus x_1 is the sophisticated outcome and x_3 and x_5 are innocuous. The sophisticated voting path is shown in Figure 13(a). For sophisticated voting under successive procedure, an alternative is innocuous if and only if it is beaten by the sophisticated equivalent in the reverse path leading from the final decision node to the initial node; this implies that every alternative that precedes the voting outcome in the voting order is innocuous.

Sophisticated Voting Under Amendment Procedure   The sophisticated equivalent agenda under amendment procedure is the least self-eivident of the four. Examination of an amendment agenda tree shows that alternative x_m can survive as the sophisticated equivalent all the way up to the initial node if and only if it beats every other alternative. Alternative x_{m-1} can become a sophisticated equivalent only if it beats x_m; and it can survive as a sophisticated equivalent all the way up to the initial node if and only if it beats all other alternatives that beat x_m. Alternative x_{m-2} can become a sophisticated equivalent only if it beats x_m and, if x_{m-1} beats x_m, also x_{m-1}; and it can survive as a sophisticated equivalent all the way up to the initial node only it beats all other alternatives that likewise beat x_m and, if x_{m-1} beats x_m, also x_{m-1}. Extending this logic, the *sophisticated equivalent agenda under amendment procedure* is defined by backwards induction as:

$$z_m = x_m; \text{ and for all } m - 1 \geq h \geq 1$$

$$z_h = \begin{cases} x_h \text{ if } x_h P z_k \text{ for all } h > k \geq m \\ z_{k+1} \text{ otherwise.}^{46} \end{cases}$$

The sophisticated equivalent agenda in Example 7 is $(z_1, ..., z_6)$ = $(x_2, x_2, x_4, x_4, x_6, x_6)$, reflecting that x_6 beats x_5 but is beaten by x_4; x_3 does not beat x_4, but x_2 beats both x_4 and x_6; x_1 beats x_6 but loses to the other elements of the sophisticated agenda. Thus x_2 is the sophisticated voting outcome, and x_1, x_3 and x_5 are innocuous. The sophisticated voting path is shown in Figure 13(b). For sophisticated voting under amendment procedure, an alternative is innocuous if and only if it fails to beat all non-innocuous alternatives that follow it in the voting order and, in particular, an alternative that precedes the voting outcome in the voting order is innocuous.

6.2. Sincere Voting Outcomes

Let us be given an agenda set A of alternatives and a voter preference profile over A. Recall that $SIN|P(A)$ designates the subset of alternatives in A

---

[46]The is the Shepsle–Weingast (1984a) sophisticated agenda algorithm, discussed in many works. Miller (1977b) earlier suggested a related method for identifying the sophisticated voting outcome under amendment procedure, as follows.

(1) Examine $P(x_m)$; if $P(x_m)$ is empty, x_m is the outcome; otherwise, the sophisticated outcome belongs to $P(x_m)$.

(2) Examine $TC[P(x_m)]$; if this top cycle is a one-element set, say $\{x_g\}$, x_g, is the outcome; otherwise, the sophisticated outcome belongs to $TC[P(x_m)]$ and depends on which alternative in this set comes last in the voting order; designate this alternative x_k.

(3) Alternative x_k cannot be the outcome; examine the intersection $P(x_k) \cap TC[P(x_m)]$ and, more particularly, the top cycle of this intersection; if this top cycle is a one-element set, say $\{x_h\}$, x_h is the outcome; otherwise, the outcome belongs to the top cycle and depends on which alternative in it comes last in the voting order.

(4) And so forth. (Since A is a finite set, and since the set of possible decisions is reduced at each stage, the method must terminate at some stage.)

Thus, in Example 7, $P(x_6)=\{x_1,x_2,x_3,x_4\}$, all the elements of which cycle. Hence the sophisticated decisions depends on which alternative in this set comes last in the voting order, i.e., x_4. Since x_4 is beaten only by x_2 in $\{x_1,x_2,x_3,x_4\}$, the outcome is x_2. Given an agenda of reasonable magnitude, this example is typical in that it is virtually never necessary to proceed beyond stage (3). Thus the method is easier to use than the Shepsle–Weingast algorithm, but it is less productive of theoretical insights. Reid (1991a, 1991b) formalizes this method and examines its relationship to the Shepsle–Weingast algorithm.

that are *possible sincere voting outcomes* under some agenda of type P. Abbreviations specifying the agenda type were given at the beginning of this section.

The principal task in this subsection is to bound or demarcate the set $SIN(A)$ for different types of agendas. We first allow *any* sequential binary agenda and set bounds on $SIN|SB(A)$.

PROPOSITION 1: *If there is a majority winner x in A, $SIN|SB(A) = \{x\}$.*

Let v be the initial decision node. Since $\Gamma(v) = A$, x belongs to $\Gamma(v)$ and also to at least one of $\Gamma(v_0)$ and $\Gamma(v_1)$. By the definition of sincere voting, if x does not belong to $\Gamma(v_0)$, the sincere voting path cannot traverse v_0, and likewise for v_1. The same pattern holds at the next node, and so forth. So the sincere voting path must lead to an outcome node giving x as the outcome.

PROPOSITION 2: *If there is a Condorcet loser x in A, x cannot belong to $SIN|SB(A)$.*

Consider any outcome node that gives y as the outcome and consider also the preceding decision node v. Then $\Gamma(v)$ contains at least two elements and either $\Gamma(v_0) = \{y\}$ or $\Gamma(v_1) = \{y\}$. By the definition of sincere voting, the sincere voting path leads to the outcome node giving y as the sincere voting outcome only if y is the majority winner, and thus, also the Condorcet winner, in $\Gamma(v)$. Therefore, if y is the outcome, y must beat at least one other alternative and cannot be a Condorcet loser in A. It does not follow that every alternative other than a Condorcet loser must belong to $SIN|SB(A)$. Indeed, we know from Proposition 1 that, if there is a majority winner, no alternative other than that winner can belong to $SIN(A|SB)$.[47] We can, however, state the following.

PROPOSITION 3: *Consider any majority preference tournament on A such that x is not a Condorcet loser. Then there is some underlying preference profile such that x is the sincere voting outcome under some sequential binary (specifically, successive) agenda.*

---

[47]Note that Proposition 2 is different from the seemingly similar result given by Ordeshook and Schwartz (1987), since (as noted in footnote 22) their definition of sincere voting is different. Given their definition, $SIN|SB(A)$ coincides with A excluding only the Condorcet loser, if any. It follows that Proposition 1 does not hold under their definition of sincere voting.

Refer back to Example 5 (in 5.1); both preference profiles entail the same majority preference tournament, in which y beats z, so y is not a Condorcet loser. Given Profile 1, the Condorcet winner x is also the majority winner and (consistent with Proposition 1) is the sincere voting outcome under any sequential binary agenda. However, given Profile 2, we can design a successive agenda (that places x first in the voting order) such that y is the sincere voting outcome. The import of Proposition 3 is that this example can always be generalized.[48]

COROLLARY 3.1: *The sincere voting outcome may fail to be an alternative in $TC(A)$ under some sequential binary (specifically, successive) agenda.*

Indeed, even if there is a Condorcet winner, it may fail to be the sincere outcome.

It follows from Example 5 that we cannot precisely demarcate *SIN|SB(A)* — or *SIN|S(A)*, *SIN|UP(A)*, or generally *SIN(A)* for any non-pairwise agenda — in terms of the majority preference tournament. However, sincere voting under successive procedure is well behaved to the following extent (Miller, 1977b).

PROPOSITION 4: *Regardless of the underlying preference profile, for every alternative x in TC(A), there is some successive agenda such that x is the sincere voting outcome; and this is true of no alternative not in TC(A).*

Recall from 5.2 that for every alternative x in $TC(A)$ there is a complete majority preference path in A beginning with x, so the alternatives may be subscripted in such a way that $x = x_m$ and $x_m P x_{m-1} P \ldots P x_2 P x_1$. Let the voting order be $x_1, \ldots, x_m$. Then at no decision node v can $\Gamma(v_0) = \{x_h\}$ be the Condorcet (let alone majority) winner in $\Gamma(v) = \{x_h, x_{h+1} \ldots, x_m\}$. Thus in the equivalent agenda, $d_h = x_h$ for all h, and x_m is the sincere voting outcome. On the other hand, given a preference profile in which there is a subset N' of voters such that (i) $|N'| \geq n/2$

---

[48]Suppose x beats y. Design a successive agenda in which, at the final decision node v', $\Gamma(v')=\{x,y\}$, and consider any prior decision node v; $\Gamma(v_0)$ is a one element set, say $\Gamma(v_0)=\{z\}$, and x and y both belong to $\Gamma(v_1)$. Let the preference profile be the one used in the proof of McGarvey's Theorem (footnote 16); then, even if z is the Condorcet winner in $\Gamma(v)$, it is not the majority winner in $\Gamma(v)$. Thus the sincere voting path reaches the final decision node, and x is the sincere decision.

and (ii) $x P_i y$ for all i in N' and for every x in $TC(A)$ and y not in $TC(A)$, no alternative not in $TC(A)$ can be the sincere outcome.

COROLLARY 4.1: *Given a successive agenda:*

(1) *the first alternative in the voting order is the sincere voting outcome only if it is the Condorcet winner; and*

(2) *if there is a Condorcet winner and it is last or next to last in the voting order, it is the sincere voting outcome.*

Sincere (and, as we shall see, sophisticated) voting outcomes tend to be most erratic — in the sense of being most powerfully dependent on the voting order — under successive agendas. Voting outcomes under *uniform* partition agendas tend to be better behaved (essentially because alternatives are more symmetrically treated); nevertheless, in the limit, we can place no tighter bound on $SIN|UP(A)$ than that given by Proposition 2. The following provides an example.

EXAMPLE 8

Preference Profile			Majority Preference Tournament	Uniform Partition Agenda

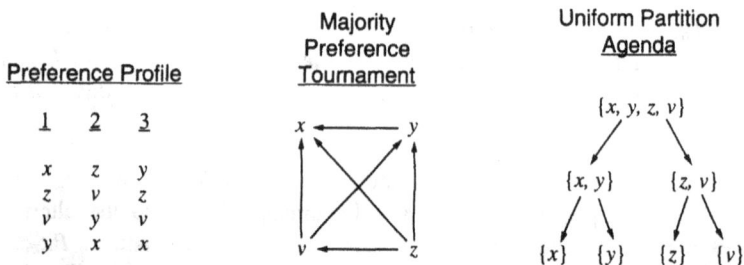

Majority preference is an ordering and y is next-to-last in this ordering, yet y is the sincere voting outcome under the agenda shown.

However, there are two other uniform partition agendas on $\{x, y, z, v\}$, which may be distinguished according to how sets of alternatives are paired at the first vote:

(1) $\{x, y\}$ vs. $\{z, v\}$ (as shown in Example 8): sincere voting outcome is y;

(2) $\{x, z\}$ vs. $\{y, v\}$: sincere voting outcome is z; and

(3) $\{x, v\}$ vs. $\{y, z\}$: sincere voting outcome is z.

The erratic nature of sincere voting under partition agendas — even those that are uniform — is further illustrated by the following example, in which $TC(A) = A$ (so there is no Condorcet winner or loser).

EXAMPLE 9

Preference Profile	Majority Preference Tournament

1	2	3	4	5
x	v	z	z	y
y	x	v	v	x
z	y	x	x	v
v	z	y	y	z

Now each possible uniform partition agenda produces a distinct sincere voting outcome:

(1) $\{x, y\}$ vs. $\{z, v\}$: sincere voting outcome is z;

(2) $\{x, z\}$ vs. $\{y, v\}$: sincere voting outcome is x; and

(3) $\{x, v\}$ vs. $\{y, z\}$: sincere voting outcome is y.

Note that v, which might be reckoned the strongest alternative (it beats the only other alternative that beats two alternatives), does not win under any such agenda. However, if voters 4 and 5 are deleted from the profile (since they have opposite preferences, the majority preference tournament is unchanged), v rather than y wins under agenda (3).

These examples show that a kind of voting order question arises under uniform partition agendas. Under an agenda of the bill-by-bill (or Plott–Levine) type, this order can be naturally interpreted in terms of the order in which 'questions' (or bills or issues) are voted on. If the alternatives in Examples 8 and 9 are labelled as they were in (the dress and cuisine) Agenda Example 7: (1) corresponds to the agenda in which the first vote is on the question of cuisine and the second on the question of dress (Figure 6(a)); (2) corresponds to the agenda in which the first vote is on the question of dress and the second is on the question of cuisine (Figure 6(b)); and (3) is not an admissible bill-by-bill type of agenda. But, in any case, we have the following.

PROPOSITION 5: *Given a uniform partition agenda of the bill-by-bill (or Plott–Levine) type, the sincere voting outcome depends on the order in which the questions are voted upon.*

Of course, the scope of Proposition 5 is limited by the more general bounds given by Propositions 1 and 2 for all sequential binary agendas.

There is an important qualification to Proposition 5, however. Suppose that voters have the preferences given in Example 8 for alternatives as labelled in Agenda Example 7. Then voter 1 prefers French to Mexican cuisine if dress is to be formal (i.e., $x P_1 z$) but prefers Mexican to French cuisine if dress is to be informal (i.e., $v P_1 y$) — that is, 1's preferences are not *separable* by questions. (Other non-separabilities also occur in the preference profile.) As suggested by the discussion in 3.4, it may often be plausible to suppose that voters do have separable preferences over the questions (issues or bills) that arise under agendas of this type. How is Proposition 5 affected if we restrict preferences in this fashion? Since the issues that arise these agendas are dichotomous, each issue has a majority position and a minority position. Let x^+ designate the alternative that includes the majority position on every issue. (Recall from 5.2 that x^+ always belongs to $TC(A)$ and thus is the Condorcet winner if one exists.)

PROPOSITION 6: *If preferences are separable by questions, $SIN|BB(A) = \{x^+\}$, so the sincere voting outcome: (a) belongs to $TC(A)$; and (b) is independent of the order in which the questions are voted on.*

Consider the initial decision node v, at which the agenda set is partitioned into the two subsets $\Gamma(v_0)$ and $\Gamma(v_1)$. By the nature of a bill-by-bill agenda, there is some issue A (the first issue to be voted on) such that every alternative in $\Gamma(v_0)$ includes the majority position on A and every alternative in $\Gamma(v_1)$ includes the minority position or *vice versa* but $\Gamma(v_0)$ and $\Gamma(v_1)$ are otherwise equivalent. Suppose that every alternative in $\Gamma(v_0)$ includes the majority position on A. Then a majority of voters must have some alternative in $\Gamma(v_0)$ as their first preference, so the sincere voting path must lead to $\Gamma(v_0)$. By similar argument, the sincere voting path must ultimately lead to the outcome node that gives the alternative x^+ that includes the majority position on every issue.[49]

---

[49] A more general result along these lines pertaining to (non-dichotomous) issue-by-issue voting is given by Kramer (1972); also see Kadane (1972).

Sincere voting outcomes are considerably better behaved under pairwise agendas than sequential binary agendas in general and partition agendas in particular.

PROPOSITION 7: $SIN|PW(A)$ *is contained in the top cycle set* $TC(A)$.

In words, only an alternative in the top cycle set can be the sincere voting outcome under any pairwise agenda.

By the pairwise nature of the agenda, the sincere voting path is driven by the majority preference tournament (and is otherwise independent of the underlying preference profile). Consider how parts of the tournament are 'revealed' as the voting path proceeds from the initial node to the node giving the sincere outcome. By the non-repetitive nature of the agenda, every alternative but one is 'revealed' to be beaten just once and there is a 'revealed' path from that one alternative to every beaten one. Thus, when the voting path reaches an outcome node, the 'revealed' majority preference tournament is a *tree* (recall the discussion in 2.3) whose initial node, from which every other node is reachable, is the sincere voting outcome. (If the pairwise agenda is also continuous, 'revealed' majority preference is a tree at every stage along the voting path.) Since this tree is a subrelation of the full tournament, every alternative is reachable from the sincere outcome in the full tournament as well. Hence (by results given in 5.2) the outcome must belong to $TC(A)$.[50]

COROLLARY 7.1: *If there is a Condorcet winner* x *in* A, $SIN|PW(A) = \{x\}$.

For amendment agendas, the following proposition, in conjunction with the preceding one, tells us that $SIN|A(A) = TC(A)$.

PROPOSITION 8: *For every alternative* x *in* $TC(A)$, *there is some amendment agenda such that* x *is the sincere voting outcome.*

As in the manner of the proof of Proposition 4, let the voting order be the reverse of the complete majority preference path beginning with any x in $TC(A)$ that we know exists. From the sincere equivalent agenda under amendment procedure, it follows that x is the outcome (Miller, 1977b).

---

[50]This generalizes the proof given in Miller (1977b) for amendment agendas; also see Kramer (1977).

In Anglo-American voting bodies, two circumstances commonly lead to departures from standard amendment agendas. First, if two (or more) or first-order amendments are introduced, the agenda is rendered incomplete. Since the resulting agenda is non-pairwise, Propositions 7 and 8 do not apply. Consider Agenda Example 6 (and Figure 5), relabelling the alternatives in this more concise fashion: $x = m$, $y = m+a_1$, $z = m+a_2$, $v = m+a_1+a_2$, and $q = \phi$.

EXAMPLE 10

Majority Preference Tournament

Preference Profile

1	2	3
z	y	x
v	v	q
y	x	v
x	q	y
q	z	z

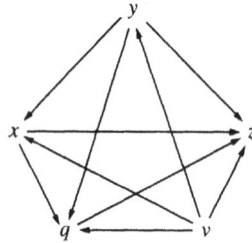

Since voter 1 most prefers z and voter 3 most prefers x and both of these alternatives entail defeat of the first amendment, a_1 is defeated; since x beats both z and q, x (the unamended motion) is the sincere voting outcome, although v (the motion with both amendments attached is the Condorcet winner. This comes about because we have a partition 'amendment-by-amendment' subagenda 'standardized' by a final vote against the status quo. Since Proposition 5 applies within the subagenda, the sincere voting outcome depends on the order in which the amendments are voted on. If the agenda were modified so that a_2 were voted on first, a_1 would pass and y would be the sincere voting outcome. Note that preferences in Example 10 are not separable by amendments. Proposition 6 applies to the subagenda as well — that is, if preferences are separable by amendments, the sincere voting outcome from such an agenda belongs to $TC(A)$ and is independent of the order in which the amendments are voted on.

The other common departure from a standard amendment agenda results from substitute bills, in the manner of Agenda Example 5. Since a two-stage amendment agenda is pairwise, Propositions 7 holds. However, it is discontinuous, so Proposition 8 does not apply. Recall that under a two-stage amendment agenda, the full agenda set A = is partitioned into three subsets: A^1, the original bill and its amended variants; A^2, the substitute bill and its amended variants, and A^3, a one-element set including only the status quo. Let us subscript the alternatives such that $A^1 = \{x_1, ..., x_{h-1}\}$, $A^2 = \{x_h, ..., x_{m-1}\}$, and $A^3 = \{x_m\}$.

We may note that if A^2 is a one-element set and the voting order in A^1 is indicated by the subscripts, the resulting two-stage amendment agenda is identical to the (one-stage) amendment agenda with the voting order x_1, $x_2, \ldots, x_m$; and if A^1 is a one-element set and the voting order in A^2 is indicated by the subscripts, the resulting two-stage amendment agenda is identical to the amendment agenda with the voting order $x_2, \ldots x_{m-1}, x_1, x_m$. Thus, corresponding to any standard (one-stage) amendment agenda is some 'degenerate' two-stage amendment agenda, in which either the bill or the substitute has no proposed amendments; it follows from this and previous propositions that $SIN|A2(A) = SIN|A(A) = TC(A)$.

Let us therefore focus attention on *non-degenerate* two-stage amendment agendas (such that A^1 and A^2 both have at least two elements) structurally distinct from any one-stage amendment agenda. Let $SIN|A2^*(A)$ designate the set of possible sincere outcomes under such agendas. Given that both A^1 and A^2 have two or more elements, an alternative in either A^1 or A^2 can be the sincere voting outcome only if it beats at least three other alternatives, i.e., one in each of A^1 and A^2 and the unique element in A^3. And the unique element in A^3 is the sincere voting outcome only if beats some alternative that in turn beats two other alternatives, i.e., the winner of the winners from A^1 and A^2. Thus we have the following.

PROPOSITION 9: *An alternative x belongs to $SIN|A2^*(A)$ only if (a) $|P^{-1}(x)| \geq 3$ or (b) there is some y in A such that $x P y$ and $|P^{-1}(y)| \geq 2$.*

Since they may fail to meet both (a) and (b), alternatives in $TC(A)$ may fail to belong to $SIN|A2^*(A)$.

Suppose now that a (possibly degenerate) partition is fixed as A^g, A^h, and $A^3 = \{x_m\}$. What is not fixed is whether $A^g = A^1$ and $A^h = A^2$ or *vice versa* and what the voting order is with each of A^g and A^h. Let $SIN|A2(A:A^g, A^h)$ designate the set of possible sincere outcomes when $A^g = A^1$ and $A^h = A^2$. By Proposition 7, the preliminary outcome from A^g belongs to $TC(A^g)$ and the preliminary outcome from A^h belongs to $TC(A^h)$, so the final outcome belongs to one of these two sets or is the status quo x_m. Whether this allows any alternative in $TC(A)$ to become the outcome depends on whether $TC(A)$ is contained in a single element of the partition or intersects two or more elements. If $TC(A)$ is contained in A^k for some $k = 1, 2, 3$ (as is certainly true if there is a Condorcet winner), $TC(A^k) = TC(A)$, the final outcome must belong to $TC(A^k)$ and, by a straightforward generalization of Proposition 8, any element of $TC(A^k) = TC(A)$ may be the outcome, given an appropriate order of voting within A^k. However, if $TC(A)$ intersects but is not contained in A^k, $TC(A^k)$ is a subset of that intersection — most likely, but not certainly, a proper subset (if A^k has two or more elements). Thus $SIN|A2(A:A^g, A^h)$ may be a proper subset of $TC(A)$. Finally, it is apparent that, under sincere voting, A^1 and A^2 are treated symmetrically (just as are the first two alternatives in the voting order under amendment procedure), so $SIN|A2(A:A^g, A^h) = SIN|A2(A:A^h, A^g)$. Example 11 illustrates these points.

EXAMPLE 11

Majority Preference Tournament

$TC(A) = \{x, y, z, v, w\}$
$A^g = \{x, y, z\}$
$A^h = \{v, w\}$

status quo (not shown) is
Condorcet loser

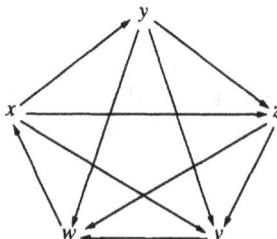

Note that $SIN|A2(A) = TC(A) = \{x, y, z, v, w\}$ but, by Proposition 9, v cannot belong to $SIN|A2^*(A)$ (and w can win only in the role of the status quo). However, once the partition is fixed as shown, $TC(A^g) = \{x\}$, $TC(A^h) = \{v\}$, and xPv, so x is the only possible sincere voting outcome.

We conclude by noting the following self-evident proposition, where x_0 is the status quo.

PROPOSITION 10: *Under any standard agenda, SIN(A) is contained in* $\bar{P}(x_0)$.

6.3. Sophisticated Voting Outcomes

Let us be given an agenda set A and a preference profile over A. Let $SOPH|P(A)$ designate the subset of alternatives in A that are *possible sophisticated voting outcomes* under a specified category P of agendas, using the same abbreviations as before.

A basic conclusion is that sophisticated voting is better behaved than sincere, in that there are generally tighter bounds on $SOPH(A)$ than $SIN(A)$. For example, the bound on $SOPH(A)$ for all sequential binary procedures is the same as the bound on $SIN(A)$ for pairwise procedures.

PROPOSITION 11: $SOPH|SB(A)$ *is contained in* $TC(A)$.

Consider any alternative x in $TC(A)$, some outcome node v such that $\Gamma(v) = \{x\}$, and the reverse path leading from v to the initial node. Alternative x is the sophisticated equivalent at v. At any preceding node traversed by the path, x can be displaced as the sophisticated equivalent only by some other alternative y that beats x. Alternative y in turn can be displaced only by some other alternative that beats y. And so forth. Thus either x or some alternative in $\mathcal{P}(x)$ is the sophisticated equivalent at the initial node, and therefore the sophisticated voting outcome must belong to $TC(X)$ (Miller, 1977b; McKelvey and Niemi, 1978).

COROLLARY 11.1: *If there is a Condorcet winner* x *in* A, $SOPH|SB(A) = \{x\}$.

If we consider any standard agenda and imagine that every final decision node is removed, Proposition 11 gives us the following.

PROPOSITION 12: *Given any standard agenda in which the status quo* x_0 *is not the Condorcet winner, the sophisticated voting decision belongs to* $TC[P(x_0)]$.

For sophisticated voting behavior as well as sincere, voting outcomes are most erratic under successive agendas. In particular, no bounds can be placed on $SOPH|S(A)$ tighter than those given by Proposition 11 for binary agendas in general.

PROPOSITION 13: *For every alternative* x *in* $TC(A)$, *there is some successive agenda such that* x *is the sophisticated voting outcome*.

This follows from Proposition 8 in conjunction with the reversibility property relating sophisticated voting under successive procedure with sincere voting under amendment procedure (recall 6.1). It follows that Proposition 11 can be strengthened as follows.

PROPOSITION 11′: *SOPH|SB(A) coincides with TC(A).*

Under uniform partition agendas, sophisticated voting outcomes are somewhat more constrained and a slightly tighter bound can be given.

PROPOSITION 14: *Given a uniform partition agent in which k votes are taken, an alternative x belongs to SOPH|UP(A) only if $|P^{-1}(x)| \geq k$.*

Suppose x is the sophisticated outcome. Thus x is the sophisticated equivalent at every node traversed by the reverse path leading from the (unique) outcome node (of order k) giving x to the initial node. Since k other (reverse) paths merge with this one, x must beat the k other sophisticated equivalents, which — given the partition nature of the agenda — are all distinct from x and each other. Thus x must beat at least k other alternatives. Since an alternative in $TC(A)$ may beat no more than one other alternative, the necessary condition given in Proposition 14 is independent of that given in Proposition 11. For example, given the majority preference tournament in Example 9 (in which $TC(A) = A$), $SOPH|UP(A) = \{x, v\}$.

If a uniform partition agenda is a bill-by-bill (or Plott–Levine) agenda, and if preferences are separable, the same constraint applies to sophisticated as to sincere voting outcomes.

PROPOSITION 15: *If preferences are separable by questions, SOPH| BB(A) = $\{x^+\}$, so the sophisticated voting outcome is independent of the order in which the questions are voted on.*

As reverse paths leading from outcome nodes to the initial node merge, sophisticated equivalents differ with respect to just one issue, so the sophisticated equivalent including the majority position on that issue prevails and, in particular, x^+ prevails as a sophisticated equivalent to the top of the tree and is the sophisticated outcome.[51]

---

[51] See Ferejohn (1975) and also Kadane (1972). Such an agenda with separable preferences provides an example of what Austen-Smith (1987) calls 'sophisticated sincerity,' in that every voter's sophisticated strategy is also sincere.

Let us now consider the majority preference tournament shown in Example 9 and all possible amendment agendas. Using the sophisticated equivalent agenda for amendment procedure, it may be checked that, regardless of the earlier part of the voting order, if v is last in the voting order, z is the sophisticated outcome; if z is last, x is the outcome; if y is last, v is the outcome; and if x last, v is the outcome.[52] Thus, though y belongs to $TC(A)$, y does not belong to $SOPH|A(A)$. We may note that y is covered by x and $SOPH|A(A) = UC(A)$ in this example. Miller (1980) showed that $SOPH|A(A)$ is always a subset of $UC(A)$. Banks (1985) subsequently observed that the sophisticated equivalent agenda algorithm (due to Shepsle and Weingast, 1984a) allows a precise characterization of $SOPH|A(A)$ — namely, what we identified in 5.4 as the Banks set — and he showed that this set in general is smaller than $UC(A)$.

PROPOSITION 16: $SOPH|A(A)$ coincides with $B(A)$.

To demonstrate this, we need only to observe that, given any voting order, the resulting sophisticated equivalent agenda under amendment procedure (more precisely, the truncated version in which repetitions are deleted) is a Banks chain. Thus its top element, which is the sophisticated voting outcome, is a Banks alternative. Referring to Example 7, we saw that the sophisticated equivalent agenda is $(x_2, x_2, x_4, x_4, x_6, x_6)$, so its truncated version is (x_2, x_4, x_6) — a Banks chain with bottom element x_6 and top element x_2. Considering all possible voting orders, we construct all possible Banks chains, so $SOPH|SA(A) = B(A)$.

COROLLARY 16.1: $SOPH|A(A)$ is a subset of $UC(A)$ and thus also of $PO(A)$.

As was demonstrated by Example 6, $TC(A)$ may include Pareto-dominated alternatives. It follows from Proposition 8 that Pareto-dominated alternative may be the sincere voting outcome under some amendment agendas. Sophisticated voting precludes this seemingly perverse possibility.

COROLLARY 16.2: *Alternative x belongs to $SOPH|A(A)$ only if every other alternative is reachable from x by a path of no more than two steps.*

---

[52] Actually, these conclusions may be reached most readily by the alternate algorithm described in footnote 46 (or by Proposition 12), since in each case the outcome may be identified once the last alternative in the voting order is specified.

We turn now to sophisticated voting outcomes under two-stage amendment procedure, definitively analyzed by Banks (1989). We can, of course, determine sophisticated voting outcomes from such agendas by the generic method of constructing the agenda tree and determining sophisticated equivalents up to the initial node. But a more productive method exploits the fact that a two-stage amendment agenda is composed of several standard amendment agendas.[53]

Consider a two-stage amendment agenda with alternatives subscripted in the order in which they first enter the voting, so that $A^1 = \{x_1, \ldots, x_h\}$, $A^2 = \{x_{h+1}, \ldots, x_{m-1}\}$, and $A^3 = \{x_m\}$. Figure 14 shows part of such an agenda tree with $A^1 = \{x_1, x_2, x_3\}$, $A^2 = \{x_4, x_5\}$, and $A^3 = \{x_6\}$. The *preliminary* subagenda is the agenda tree through each node of order $h - 1$ (order 2 in Figure 14), by means of which the original bill is perfected.

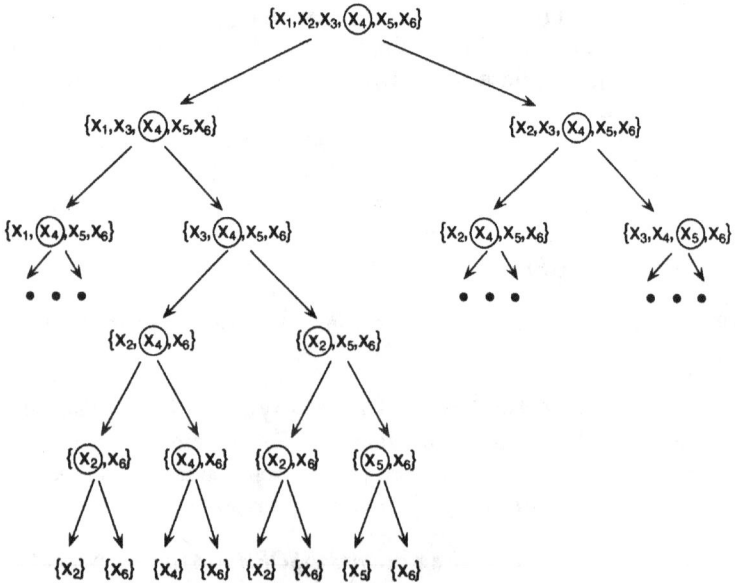

FIGURE 14 Part of a Two-stage Amendment Agenda

[53]The following discussion is adapted from Banks (1989).

Beginning with each terminal node of the preliminary subagenda is a *secondary* subagenda (only one of which is shown in Figure 14), by means of which the substitute bill is perfected, a choice is made between the perfected bill and the perfected substitute, and the surviving version of the bill is accepted or rejected. Thus each secondary subagenda is equivalent to a standard amendment agenda on $m - h + 1$ alternatives with the voting order $x_{h+1}, \ldots, x_{m-1}, x_g, x_m$, where x_g is the perfected version of the original bill and each secondary subagenda is identical except for the identity of x_g.[54] We can determine the sophisticated voting outcome for each secondary subagenda, i.e., for each x_g in A^1, and designate the corresponding, outcome $d(x_g)$. Note that, in the full agenda tree, $s(v) = d(x_g)$ at the node v that is the initial node of a secondary subagenda that includes x_g. We now replace the reachable set $\Gamma(v) = \{x_g, x_h, \ldots, x_m\}$ at each terminal node v of the preliminary subagenda with $s(v) = d(x_g)$. This gives us the *reduced two-stage agenda* with agenda set A^r, where A^r is the set of outcomes $d(x_g)$ for all x_g in A^1. The *structure* of this reduced agenda is given by the preliminary subagenda; its *content* is given by A^r. Finally, we determine the sophisticated voting outcome from this reduced agenda, which is the sophisticated voting outcome from the overall two-stage amendment agenda.

This analysis may be illustrated by the two-stage agenda shown in Figure 14 inconjunction with the following preferences.

EXAMPLE 12

Majority

Preference

Tournament

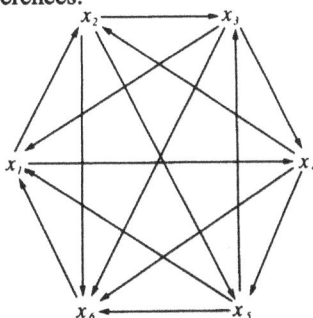

The preliminary agenda is shown in Figure 15(a) It may be checked that $d(x_1) = x_4$, $d(x_2) = x_4$, and $d(x_3) = x_5$. The reduced agenda is shown in Figure 15(b); note that the redundancy by which both x_1 and x_2 are replaced by x_4 causes no problem. We see that the sophisticated voting outcome is x_4.

---

[54]Given a *conditional* two-stage amendment agenda, the secondary subagendas may also differ with respect to the voting order. With this qualification, we can still proceed in the manner described to determine the sophisticated voting decision (Banks, 1989).

From this analysis, we derive several propositions.

PROPOSITION 17A: *The status quo x_m belongs to SOPH|A2(A) if and only if x_m is the Condorcet winner.*

Sufficiency follows from Corollary 11.1. To demonstrate necessity, we observe that if x_m is beaten by any z in A^2, x_m cannot be the sophisticated outcome from any secondary subagenda, thus does not belong to A^r, and cannot be the sophisticated outcome from the overall agenda. Suppose, however, that x_m beats everything in A_2, but is beaten by some y in A^1; then y is the sophisticated outcome from any secondary agenda including y and, in general, every element of A^r distinct from x_m beats x_m. So x_m cannot be the sophisticated outcome from the reduced agenda nor, in turn, from the overall agenda.

PROPOSITION 17B: *If x_m is not the Condorcet winner, SOPH|A2(A) is contained in $P(x_m)$.*

An alternative that fails to beat x_m is innocuous in each secondary agenda, therefore does not belong A^r, and cannot be the sophisticated outcome.[55]

COROLLARY 17.1: *If x_m is not the Condorcet winner and $A' = A \cap P(x_m)$, then SOPH|A2(A) = SOPH|A2(A').*

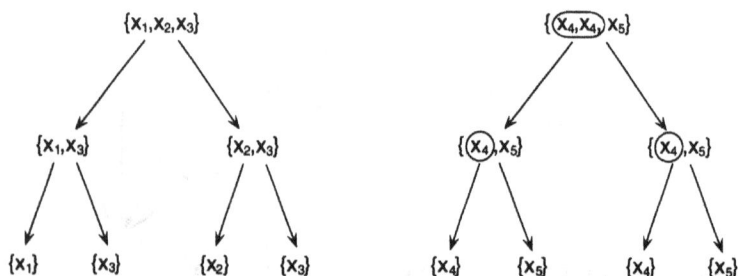

(a) The Preliminary Agenda For Example 12   (b) The Reduced Agenda For Example 12

FIGURE 15

---

[55] Proposition 17B is also a corollary of Proposition 12.

More generally, provided x_m is not the Condorcet winner, we can analyze sophisticated voting given a two-stage amendment agenda on A as if the agenda were restricted to the subset A' of alternatives on the agenda that beat x_m. Put otherwise, we may suppose the set A' is partitioned into subsets $A^{1'}$ and $A^{2'}$, a preliminary choice is made from an amendment agenda on each subset, and a choice is made between the two preliminary outcomes.

Continuing to follow Banks (1989), we now give several conditions for an alternative to be the sophisticated voting outcome under two-stage amendment procedure. Recall that a subset X' of alternatives is *externally stable* in X if every alternative in $X - X'$ is beaten by some alternative in X'. X' is a *minimal* externally stable set if it has no proper subset that is also externally stable. An alternative in a minimal externally stable set X' either (i) beats every other alternative in X' (clearly true of at most one element of X') or (ii) uniquely (with respect to the elements of X') beats some alternative in $X - X'$.

PROPOSITION 18: *Alternative x belongs to SOPH|A2(A) if (1) $\{x\} = A^3$ and x is the Condorcet winner in A, or (2) x belongs to UC(A'), or (3) x belongs to $B(A'')$ for some minimal externally stable subset A'' in A'.*

The sufficiency of (1) has already been demonstrated. To demonstrate the sufficiency of (2), we set $A^{1'}$ equal to $\bar{P}(x) \cap A'$, i.e., x together with everything in A' that beats x, and $A^{2'}$ equal to $P^{-1}(x) \cap A'$, i.e., everything in A' that x beats. It follows that for every secondary agenda containing x, $d(x) = x$. But since x is uncovered in A', every y in A^1 other than x is beaten by something in $A^{2'}$, so, for all such y, $d(y) = z$, where z belongs to $A^{2'}$. Hence A^r includes only x and alternatives x beats, and x must be the sophisticated outcome from the reduced agenda, whatever its voting order, and likewise from the overall agenda. To demonstrate the sufficiency of (3), we set $A^{2'}$ equal to A''. Since A'' is externally stable, A^r is a subset of A''. Since A'' is a minimal externally stable set in A', either (i) every alternative in A^2 except one uniquely beats some element of $A^{1'}$, or (ii) every alternative in $A^{2'}$ uniquely beats some element of $A^{1'}$. Suppose (i) holds and x is the exceptional alternative. Then x beats every other alternative in $A^{2'}$ and is therefore uncovered in A' (since every alternative in $A^{1'}$ is beaten by some alternative in $A^{2'}$), and x belongs to $SOPH|A2(A)$ by the sufficiency of (2). Suppose (ii) holds. Then $A^{2'} = A^r$. Since x belongs to $B(A'')$, there is some voting order for the preliminary agenda such that x is the sophisticated voting outcome from the reduced, and therefore the overall, agenda.

COROLLARY 18.1: *SOPH|A2(A) is in general more inclusive than SOPH|A(A).*[56]

Still following Banks (1989), we also establish necessary conditions for alternatives to be possible sophisticated voting outcomes under two-stage amendment procedure when the partition has been fixed but not the voting order within each element of the partition. We designate this set $SOPH|A2(A:A^1, A^2)$. As before, $A' = A \cap P(x_m)$, $A^{1'} = A^1 \cap P(x_m)$, and $A^{2'} = A^2 \cap P(x_m)$.

PROPOSITION 19:

   (1)   Alternative x in $A^{1'}$ belongs to $SOPH|A2(A:A^{1'}, A^{2'})$ only if (i) $x P z$ for all z in $A^{2'}$ and (ii) x belongs to $UC(A')$.

   (2)   Alternative x in $A^{2'}$ belongs to $SOPH|A2(A:A^{1'}, A^{2'})$ only if (i) $A^{2'}$ is externally stable in A', (ii) $x P y$ for some y in $A^{1'}$, and (iii) x belongs to $UC(A^{2'})$.

To demonstrate the necessity of (i) in (1), suppose there is some z in $A^{2'}$ such that $z P x$; then $d(x) \neq x$, so x does not belong to A^r and cannot be the outcome. To demonstrate the necessity of (ii) in (1), suppose there is some y in A' that covers x; if y belongs to A^2, x cannot be the outcome by (i); if y belongs to $A^{1'}$, $d(x) = x$ implies $d(y) = y$ so, if x belongs to A^r, y does also, and x cannot be the sophisticated outcome from the reduced, or overall, agenda.

To demonstrate the necessity of (i) in (2), suppose $A^{2'}$ is not externally stable in A', i.e., that there is some non-empty subset $A^{1''}$ in $A^{1'}$ such that $z P y$ for all z in $A^{1''}$ and all y in $A^{2'}$; then $A^{1''}$ is a subset of A^r and $A^{1''} = TC(A^r)$, so the sophisticated outcome cannot be outside of $A^{1''}$. (This demonstrates that (i) in (1) is not only necessary for a given x in $A^{1''}$ but is sufficient for some such x.) If neither (ii) nor (iii) in (2) holds, x does not belong to A^r, and cannot be the sophisticated outcome.

COROLLARY 19.1: *SOPH|A2(A:A^1, A^2) is contained in $A^{2'}$ if $A^{2'}$ is externally stable in A' and is contained in $A^{1'}$ otherwise.*

Proposition 19 shows that, in contrast to the result for sincere voting, in general $SOPH|A2(A:A^g, A^h) \neq SOPH|A2(A:A^h, A^g)|$ and it is easier for alternatives in A^2 to win than for those in A^1.

COROLLARY 19.2: $SOPH|A2(A:A^g, A^h) = SOPH|A2(A:A^h, A^g)$ *only if exactly one of* $A^{g'}$ *or* $A^{h'}$ *is externally stable in* A'.

The following result parallels Corollary 16.2 for one-stage amendment procedure.

COROLLARY 19.3: *Alternative* x *belongs to* $SOPH|A2(A)$ *only if every other alternative in* A *is reachable from* x *by a path of no more than three steps.*

If $\{x\} = A^3$, x is the Condorcet winner, and every other alternative is reachable by a path of one step. Otherwise x belongs to A'. The status quo x_m by definition of A' is reachable from any x in A' by a path of one step and any alternative in $P^{-1}(x_m)$ is reachable from any x in A' by a path of no more than two steps. If x belongs to $A^{2'}$, it also belongs to $UC(A^{2'})$, so any other alternative in $A^{2'}$ is reachable by a path of no more than two steps and, since $A^{2'}$ is externally stable in A', any alternative in $A^{1'}$ is reachable by a path of no more than three steps. If x belongs to $A^{1'}$, it also belongs to $UC(A')$, so any other alternative in A' is reachable by a path of no more than two steps.

6.4. Order-of-Voting Effects

It is commonly appreciated that the position of an alternative in the voting order may affect whether it becomes the voting outcome. This in turn implies that the order in which proposals are made — and accordingly their parliamentary status as original motion, amendment, substitute, etc. — influences the voting outcome.

According to Black (1958: p. 40), 'when... [amendment] procedure is in use, the later any motion enters the voting, the greater its chance of adoption.' Since the voting order under amendment procedure is typically the reverse of the order in which the alternatives were proposed, this implies that it is advantageous to make a proposal as early as possible. Farquharson (1969a: p. 62) agrees with Black that 'if voting is sincere [as Black assumed], the later a proposal is voted on, the better its chance [under either amendment or successive procedure],' but he further asserts that 'if voting is sophisticated, the earlier a proposal is voted on, the better its chance.'

These assertions are imprecise. First, once the agenda, preference profile, and behavioral assumption are fixed, a given alternative either will, or will not, become the voting outcome — 'chance' is not involved. Second, whether a given alternative x becomes the voting outcome depends (in general) on the entire voting order (or much of it), not just on the position of x in that order. The statements of Black and Farquharson are misleading in so far as they may suggest that an alternative in $SIN(A)$ (or $SOPH(A)$) must be the outcome if it is last (or first) in the voting order or that, if x wins under some order in which it is in the k th position, it therefore wins under any such voting order. Consider the preference profile in Example 9 in conjunction with sincere voting under amendment procedure. $SIN|A(A) = \{x, y, z, v\}$ but, given the voting order z, v, x, y, the sincere voting outcome is x, not y. Moreover, if the voting order is changed to y, z, v, x — which puts x later in the order than before — x is no longer the sincere outcome.

Clearly, what Black and Farquharson were saying was that an alternative is favored under sincere (sophisticated) voting if it comes later (earlier) rather than earlier (later) in the voting order, *provided the voting order otherwise remains the same.*[57] In fact, recent results by Jung (1990), which follow directly from the sincere and sophisticated equivalent agendas for these two procedures, show that considerably stronger propositions hold.

PROPOSITION 20: *Given either an amendment or successive agenda, if alternative x, in the h th position in the voting order, is the sincere voting outcome, x is also the sincere voting outcome under any other voting order that is identical with respect to the first $(h − 1)$ positions.*

---

[57] Even this is not totally precise. The most obvious sense in which alternative x can come later in the voting order, while the order otherwise remains the same, is for x to 'leap ahead' of several other alternatives, each of which drops back by one position. This definition is used by Niemi and Gretlein (1985) in their 'precise restatement of Black's theorem on voting orders,' and by Niemi and Rasch (1987) its extension to successive procedure. Another sense in which alternative x can come later in the voting order, while the order otherwise remains the same, is for x to be 'switched' with an (initially) later alternative y in the order, all other alternatives remaining in the same position. In principle, the 'switching' sense is more general, since any 'leaping' change can be accomplished by successive 'switches' of adjacent alternatives. The recent work by Jung (1990), discussed just below, sidesteps this ambiguity.

COROLLARY 20.1: *If there is no amendment or successive agenda that puts last x last in the voting order which yields x as the sincere voting outcome, there is no such agenda whatsoever that yields x as the sincere outcome.*

PROPOSITION 21: *Given either an amendment or successive agenda, if alternative x, in the hth position in the voting order, is the sophisticated voting outcome, it is also the sophisticated voting outcome under any other voting order that is identical with respect to the last $(h + 1)$ positions.*

COROLLARY 21.1: *If there is no amendment or successive agenda that puts last x first in the voting order that yields x as the sophisticated voting outcome, there is no such agenda whatsoever that yields x as the sophisticated outcome.*

Another way to verify Black and Farquharson's assertions is to hold the agenda constant and vary the type of voting behavior. We let subscripts indicate the order of voting, so that x_m is last in the voting order and x_g precedes x_h if and only $g < h$.

PROPOSITION 22: *Under a given successive agenda, if x_h and $x_{h'}$ are distinct alternatives and are the sincere and sophisticated voting outcomes, respectively, x_h follows $x_{h'}$ in the order of voting, i.e., $h' < h$.*

Suppose to the contrary that $h < h'$. But then the sincere equivalent agenda implies that $x_h P x_{h'}$, while the sophisticated equivalent agenda implies that $x_{h'} P x_h$. Thus we must have $h' < h$ (Miller, 1977b).

PROPOSITION 23: *Under a given amendment agenda, if x_h and $x_{h'}$ are distinct alternatives and are sincere and sophisticated voting outcomes, respectively, x_h follows $x_{h'}$ in the order of voting, i.e., $h' < h$. Moreover, $x_{h'} P x_h$.*

Suppose to the contrary that $h < h'$. But then the sincere equivalent agenda implies that $x_h P z$ for all z in $\{x_{h+1}, \ldots, x_m\}$, while the sophisticated equivalent agenda implies that some subset of $\{x_{h'}, \ldots, x_m\}$ in turn a subset of $\{x_{h+1}, \ldots, x_m\}$, is an externally stable (Banks) chain, which implies that $z P x_h$ for some z in $\{x_{h+1}, \ldots, x_m\}$. Thus we must have $h' < h$. Moreover, since $x_h P z$ for all z in $\{x_{h+1}, \ldots, x_m\}$, as we build a chain working from x_m back up the voting order, in the manner entailed by the sophisticated equivalent agenda, x_h must be an element of this chain. In due course, we assemble the Banks chain with top element $x_{h'}$, so $x_{h'} P x_h$.[58]

It may be worthwhile to recall explicitly that, except for sincere voting under successive procedure, order-of-voting effects depend entirely on intransitivities in majority preference and, in particular, if there is a Condorcet winner, it is the voting outcome regardless of the order of voting.

6.5. Cooperative Voting Outcomes

If voters can coordinate their voting strategies, the voting outcome depends on what coalition agreement is made and carried out. As we saw in 4.6, what agreement is ultimately made depends on the external vulnerability (or invulnerability) of potential agreements, which in turn depends only on the majority preference tournament and is independent of the particular procedure or voting order that is being used.[59] Accordingly, the set $COOP(A)$ of possible cooperative voting outcomes from agenda set A never needs to be specified — in the manner of $SIN(A)$ or $SOPH(A)$ — with respect to the procedure in use. Moreover, if $COOP(A)$ contains several alternatives, this comes about, not because different voting orders may be used, but because of intrinsic indeterminacy regarding what coalition agreement will be reached.

As we saw in 4.6, a coalition agreement that gives an outcome beaten in majority preference is externally vulnerable and unlikely to endure. This consideration seems to imply that, if there is a Condorcet winner x^* in A, $COOP(A) = \{x^*\}$; but it leaves unclear what $COOP(A)$ will be in the absence of a Condorcet winner. More detailed consideration of cooperative voting may at first cast doubt on our expectation concerning $COOP(A)$ given a Condorcet winner, but such consideration ultimately confirms our expectation and also largely resolves the problem of demarcating $COOP(A)$ even in the absence of a Condorcet winner. Consider the following example.

---

[58] These points are proved in Miller (1977b) but considerably more tortuously, as the voting algorithms presented in 6.1 were not then unavailable to be invoked; also see Reid (1991a). It is easy to construct examples showing that $x'_h P x_h$ does not hold for successive procedure.

[59] We continue to assume a simple voting body using the majority vote counting rule at every decision node; see footnote 32.

EXAMPLE 13

Preference Profile   Majority Preference Tournament

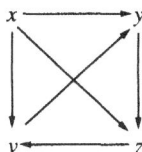

1	2	3
y	v	z
x	x	x
z	y	v
v	z	y

Suppose some majority (or unanimous) coalition has agreed to coordinate strategies in a way that would give x as the outcome. Whatever coalition is involved, this agreement is externally invulnerable; whoever the outsider (if any) is, he cannot offer an agreement to a member of the coalition that gives an outcome that both the outsider and the coalition member prefer to x. Thus no replacement agreement can be made, and we expect the initial agreement to endure.

Now suppose the attention of some majority coalition were focused on a different alternative. Suppose in particular that the coalition $\{1, 2\}$ had agreed to coordinate strategies in a way that would give y as the outcome. In this event, the outsider 3 can offer an agreement to 2 to make x the outcome *or* an agreement to make v the outcome. Both voters prefer the outcomes given by both possible agreements to y, but the first proposal is especially good for 3 and the second is especially good for 2. Thus there may appear to be a potential bargaining deadlock between 3 and 2, so that it is not clear that a replacement agreement will be made or, if it is, whether it will give x or v as the outcome. The possible deadlock is more transparent at the level of majority preference; the agreement on y is externally vulnerable but, since y is beaten by both v and x, it may not be immediately clear whether the agreement giving y would be replaced by one giving x or one giving v. And if a replacement agreement giving v is a possibility, then in like manner subsequent replacement agreements might cycle indefinitely through the 'bottom cycle' $yPzPvPy$, so that no agreement on the Condorcet winner would ever be reached. Thus our expectation that $COOP(A) = \{x\}$ would not be borne out.

But, if we look further at the majority preference tournament, we see the claims of agreements giving x and v, respectively, to replace an agreement on y are not equally strong because, while x and v both belong to $P(y)$, it is also true that $x P v$. We can return to the level of individual interactions to see how this fact plays out. Looking more broadly at the preference profile, we see that in fact there is no potential for a bargaining deadlock between 3 and 2 and that the replacement agreement will in fact give x. For suppose voter 2 tries to insist on an agreement with 3 giving v as the outcome. Voter 3 has no reason to give in to this demand, because he can readily turn to voter 1 to make an agreement giving x, since both 3 and 1 prefer x to v. Indeed, if voter 3 did not take this initiative, voter 1 — faced with the worst possible outcome by the proposal 2 is pressing on 3 — would surely initiate the counter-proposal for x. On the other hand, if voter 3 presses an agreement giving x as the outcome on 2, voter 2 cannot make any counter-move. (And if 2 nevertheless does not acquiesce, so 3 and 1 move toward an agreement giving x, there is again nothing 2 can do to preempt this.)

Thus we expect an initial agreement giving y (or, by parallel argument, z or v) to be replaced by one giving x. Accordingly, we conclude that, if the initial coalition agreement does not give x, its immediate replacement will, so indeed $COOP(A) = \{x\}$.

In general, we may suppose that any externally vulnerable agreement (or 'contract') among members of one majority coalition to make a given alternative z the voting outcome may replaced by another tentative agreement among members of another majority coalition to make some y in $P(z)$ the voting outcome. By a generalization of the argument made in connection with Example 13, we expect the replacement to be some alternative in $B(A:z)$ — that is, some top element of a Banks chain with bottom element z.[60]

This process of *recontracting* continues — generating a *recontracting path* through the majority preference tournament — until an externally invulnerable agreement is reached (i.e., an agreement on some x such that x is the Condorcet winner) or, in the absence of a Condorcet winner, until the process is broken off essentially arbitrarily (e.g., under the constraint of time). If there is a Condorcet winner x^* in A, then $\{x^*\} = B(A:z)$ for all z in $A - \{x^*\}$, so the final externally invulnerable agreement is reached in the second step of the recontracting path at the latest. Otherwise, the recontracting path never terminates but, at every step from the second onward, each agreement gives an outcome belonging to $B(A:z)$, where z is the outcome given by the prior agreement. Since $B(A:z)$ for all z in A is

---

[60] This argument is set out in more detail in Miller (1980).

a subset of $B(A)$, wherever the recontracting process broken off, the final agreement belongs to the Banks set.[61] Thus we can state the following.

PROPOSITION 24: *Under any type of agent on A, COOP(A) is a subset of B(A).*

In fact $COOP(A)$ may be more narrowly bounded, since from the third step onward the recontracting path includes only agreements giving outcomes that are top elements of Banks chains *whose bottom elements are also Banks alternatives*, and this set of alternative may be a proper subset $B^*(A)$ of $B(A)$. Moreover, from the fourth step onward the recontracting path includes only agreements giving outcomes that are top elements of Banks chains *whose bottom elements belong to $B^*(A)$*, and this set may be a proper subset $B^{**}(A)$ of $B^*(A)$. And so forth. However, his possible paring down of $B(A)$ cannot continue indefinitely; it certainly stops when we reach a set of three alternatives within which the recontracting path cycles, and it may well stop with some larger set.[62]

In conclusion, we may note that the set $COOP(A)$ is generally less relevant than $SIN(A)$ or $SOPH(A)$ to the discussion of agenda control and agenda formation in the remaining sections of this survey, because — as previously

---

[61] Miller (1980) does not use the terminology of 'Banks chains,' as this concept had not yet been identified by Banks (1985), and concludes only that $COOP(A)$ is a subset of $UC(A)$. Miller, Grofman, and Feld (1990a) make the link to Banks chains and refine the argument to conclude that $COOP(A)$ is a subset of $B(A)$.

[62] It is not possible at this time to provide an exact characterization of this solution set. However, it is closely related to — if not identical to — the *tournament equilibrium set TEQ(A)* recently proposed by Schwartz (1990) as demarcating the outcomes of cooperative majority voting. Schwartz characterizes $TEQ(A)$ axiomatically in social choice terms, but his general formulation of the problem of cooperative voting is very much in the spirit of that presented here. $TEQ(A)$ in turn is closely related, but not identical, to the 'minimal covering set' proposed by Dutta (1988, 1990); however, Dutta works within a social choice framework not particularly motivated by the problem of cooperative voting.

We may note that the solution set for cooperative voting would result from a particular reiteration of (non-cooperative) sophisticated voting on standard amendment agendas on a given agenda set A. Consider any issue entailing an agenda set A, including an initial status quo z. Suppose the issue is voted on under a standard amendment agenda and that voting is sophisticated. By the results presented in 6.4, the set of possible sophisticated voting outcomes is $B(A:z)$. Suppose that the issue is later raised again for reconsideration. Preferences remain as before, but (supposing there is no Condorcet winner in A) the parliamentary situation has changed in that there is a new status quo, i.e., the y (a Banks alternatives) in $B(A:z)$ that won initially. The new sophisticated voting outcome will be some x in $B(A:y)$. If we consider such a sequence of such reconsideration votes, the analysis exactly parallels that for cooperative voting.

noted — cooperative voting outcomes are independent of particular agenda structures.[63]

7. AGENDA CONTROL

To this point we have considered the behavior of voters and resulting voting outcomes when the agenda is exogenously fixed. In this respect, we have remained within the framework of the classical theory of voting established by Black and Farquharson. However, both the logic of the theory and practical political wisdom suggest that committee voting often plays out in an essentially mechanical fashion and that what is of greater interest and importance is how the voting agenda gets established in the first place. The common political aphorism that 'he who controls the agenda, controls the outcome' no doubt is an exaggeration, but it highlights an important limitation of the classical theory of voting. Therefore, the attention of voting theorists over the last decade or so has turned increasingly to agenda control and formation. An objective has been to make agenda formation *endogenous* to the theory of voting. The remaining sections consider efforts along these lines.

In this section and the next, we suppose that there is a distinguished member of the committee, the *agenda setter*, who: (1) may determine what sequential binary voting procedure is used; (2) may determine the order alternatives are voted on or, more or less equivalently, their parliamentary status; (3) may determine what subset of alternatives, in addition to the status quo, from the broader set X of alternatives will form the agenda set A; or (4) may be able to add alternatives to an otherwise exogenously fixed agenda set. In this section, we consider the extent to which, and the conditions under which, an agenda setter can control voting outcomes by manipulating such dimensions of the agenda. The propositions in the preceding section provide the foundation for this analysis.

---

[63] Note, however, that we have assumed that an agenda set A is exogenously given and the cooperative voters cannot make agreements outside this set. In some circumstances, it may be plausible to assume that cooperative voters can chose directly from an alternative space X (independent of any finite agenda set A). If so, other solution concepts become relevant. Though this takes us beyond the scope of the present survey, we may note briefly that, while (in the absence of a Condorcet winner) cooperative voting outcomes remain indeterminate, solution sets on alternative spaces may and typically do possess 'internal stability' — that is, they comprise sets of points that tie each other, as competitive bargaining over the alternative space focuses on pairs of alternatives between which particular voters are indifferent. An example is provided by the 'competitive solution' of McKelvey, Ordeshook, and Winer (1978).

7.1. The Scope of Agenda Control

A useful starting point for our discussion is the image of an all-powerful agenda setter suggested by some notable remarks by McKelvey (1976) (also see Plott and Levine, 1976; McKelvey, 1983) concerning implications of his global cycling theorem (discussed in 5.2).[64] McKelvey observed that, if a monopoly agenda setter knows the preferences of all voters and if voting is sincere, the agenda setter would almost always have total control over the voting outcome from an alternative space of two or more dimensions. More specifically, the agenda setter could design an agenda including any status quo x_0 and any other point x in the space such that x is the voting outcome, no matter how extreme x might be relative to the distribution of voter preferences. This picture of an omnipotent agenda setter is based on a number of restrictive assumptions, most of which McKelvey himself noted. Several of these are maintained here. But other conditions pertain to agenda structures and are more problematic.

First, the McKelvey model assumes that the agenda setter is free to use a *forward moving agenda*, under which an alternative is introduced and placed against the status quo for a vote, then a second alternative is introduced and placed against the new status quo (i.e., the winner of the first vote) for a second vote, and so forth, so the agenda is constructed as voting proceeds.[65] Under a forward moving agenda, voters really have no option but to vote sincerely at each pairwise vote. However, consistent with ordinary parliamentary practice, our standard assumption is that the whole voting agenda is constructed and known to voters before any voting begins. If the agenda setter must construct and announce an entire amendment agenda before voting begins (so that sophisticated voting is possible), we shall see that the McKelvey result holds only if voting is nevertheless sincere. (On the other hand, we shall also see that, if the agenda setter is free to use any sequential binary procedure — and a successive agenda in particular — the McKelvey result holds even if voting is sophisticated.)

Second, if the agenda must be fixed before voting begins, the McKelvey model places no constraint on the agenda setter with respect to the order in which alternatives are voted on. But standard procedure requires an agenda in which the status quo enters the voting last. We shall see that agenda control

---

[64] The following paragraphs draw from Feld, Grofman, and Miller (1989).

[65] See footnote 4.

is greatly restricted, regardless of whether voting is sincere or sophisticated, if the agenda setter is so constrained.

Third, in the McKelvey model there is no constraint on the agenda setter with respect to the number of alternatives he may place on the agenda or on how much they may differ from one another. While the global cycling theorem shows that any two points in the space are almost always linked by a cycle with a finite number of steps, it gives no sense of how large that finite number of steps may actually be. In many cases, that cycle is so long that the resulting agenda set would be unrealistically large.

The former two considerations may be simply illustrated by referring back to Example 6 (in 5.3). In this case $X = \{x, y, z, v\}$ and $TC(X) = X$ so, with respect to the finite (and small) alternative set X, we have a 'global cycle.' Suppose the status quo is z. According to the McKelvey model, for any other alternative in X, we can design an agenda such that the voting outcome is that alternative. Let v, which is no one's first preference and which fails to be Pareto-optimal, be the prospective outcome. Under a forward moving agenda, the agenda setter can pair y for a vote with the initial status quo z; y wins this vote and becomes the new status quo, which the agenda setter can pair with x, and so forth around the cycle to v. If the agenda setter must construct and announce an amendment agenda before any voting takes place but voting is nevertheless sincere, we know from Proposition 8 that the agenda setter can design an agenda — specifically, with the voting order z, y, x, v — that results in v as the sincere voting outcome. However, if the setter were limited to a standard amendment agenda that puts the status quo z last in the voting order, the required agenda is not admissible, and the possible sincere outcomes are constrained to those alternatives that beat the status quo — in this case to y alone. Moreover, if voting is sophisticated, the agenda identified above results in y as the outcome and since z covers v in X and in every subset of X including both z and v, by Corollary 16.1 there is no amendment agenda that includes z and gives v as the sophisticated outcome. However, if the agenda setter can design any sequential binary agenda, by Proposition 13 he can make v the outcome even in the face of sophisticated voting — specifically by means of a successive agenda with the voting order v, x, y, z.

This example illustrates that agenda control entails a number of complexities and certainly is not unlimited. In particular, it shows that the extent of the agenda setter's control over voting outcomes — and the particular agenda design required to effect a given outcome — depends on whether committee voting behavior is sincere or sophisticated. Of course, if voting is cooperative, outcomes are independent of the structure of the agenda. In the next subsection, we investigate the possibilities of, and limits on, agenda control in more detail and more systematically.

7.2. Control by Agenda Design

Henceforth, we consistently let x_0 designate the status quo alternative and thereafter subscript alternatives in the order in which they are generated by proposals. Thus, x_1 designates the initial motion, x_2 the motion with the first amendment, and so forth. Ordinarily, the voting order is the reverse of the order given by the subscripts; however, under a successive agenda or a forward-built amendment agenda, the voting order is that given by the subscripts. Since we need now to distinguish between standard (backward-built) amendment agendas and forward-built amendment agendas as well as between successive and sequential agendas, we designate them by SA, FB, SC, and SQ, respectively.

Fixed Agenda Set, Variable Procedure and Voting Order   Suppose that the agenda set A is fixed but that the agenda setter can design — in whole or part — the agenda structure. Under such circumstances, the scope of the agenda setter's control over voting outcomes is specified by the propositions in the previous section demarcating the set $S(A)$ for different types of agendas and voting behavior.

Thus, if the agenda setter can design any sequential binary agenda whatsoever on A, the scope of his control, under sincere and sophisticated voting, is given by $SIN|SB(A)$ and $SOPH|SB(A)$ respectively. By Proposition 11', the latter coincides with $TC(A)$. By earlier propositions, the exact size of the former depends on the preference profile underlying the majority preference tournament, but in any event $SIN|SB(A)$ is a superset of $TC(A)$ and may coincide with $A - \{z\}$, where z is the Condorcet loser in A (if any). Of course, the generosity of these bounds depends in turn on the nature of voter preferences. If voter preferences are single-peaked, or otherwise entail a Condorcet winner, Corollary 11.1 implies that the agenda setter's control over outcomes evaporates entirely if voting is sophisticated. If there is such a degree of consensus in voter preferences that a majority winner exists, Proposition 1 implies that the agenda setter's control over outcomes evaporates even if voting is sincere.

If the agenda setter is restricted to a particular type of sequential binary agenda, his control over outcomes clearly is more limited and depends importantly on the type of agenda to which he is restricted. The most generous bounds identified above result from successive (or sequential) agendas. If the agenda setter is limited to pairwise agendas, the scope of his control coincides with $TC(A)$ even if voting is sincere. If he must design an amendment agenda, the scope of his control is further constrained to $B(A)$ if voting is sophisticated.

Fixed Agenda Set, Variable Voting Order Except for Status Quo   To this point, we have ignored the consideration that one element of A represents the status quo. Since its parliamentary status is determined 'naturally,' the agenda setter may plausibly be constrained to treat the status quo x_0 in a distinctive way, by placing it last in the voting order (or first, under a successive or forward-built agenda).

Let us consider the scope of the agenda setter's control over sincere and sophisticated voting outcomes when he is constrained to use a standard amendment or sequential agenda that puts x_0 last (or a successive or forward-built amendment agenda that puts x_0 first). Let $SIN|SA(A = \{\ldots x_0\})$ and $SIN|SQ(A = \{\ldots x_0\})$ designate the set of possible sincere voting outcomes from a standard amendment agenda (Agenda Example 4a) and a sequential agenda (Agenda Example 9) on A that put x_0 last in the voting order; let $SIN|FB(A = \{x_0 \ldots\})$ and $SIN|SC(A = \{x_0 \ldots\})$ designate the set of possible sincere voting outcomes from a forward-built amendment agenda (Agenda Example 4b) and successive agenda (Agenda Example 8) on A that put x_0 first in the voting order; and likewise for other procedures and for sophisticated voting. Obviously each such set is a subset of the corresponding unconstrained set $SIN(A)$ or $SOPH(A)$. Proposition 25 demarcates or bounds these sets.

PROPOSITION 25: *If the agenda set A and the position of the status quo alternative x_0 in the voting order are fixed:*

(1) $SIN|SA(A = \{\ldots x_0\})$ *coincides with* $TC(A - \{x_0\})$ *if and only if everything in* $TC(A - \{x_0\})$ *beats* x_0, *and coincides with the intersection* $TC(A - \{x_0\}) \cap \bar{P}(x_0)$ *otherwise;*

(2) $SIN|FB(A = \{x_0 \ldots\}) = \{x_0\}$ *if and only if* x_0 *is the Condorcet winner in* A *and is a subset of* $\mathcal{P}(x_0)$ *otherwise; a sufficient condition for x to belong to* $SIN|FB(A = \{x_0 \ldots\})$ *is that there*

is a majority preference path in A from x to x_0 such that x_0 beats every alternative in A not in the path;

(3) $SIN|SQ(A = \{\ldots x_0\})$ is a superset of $SIN|SA(A = \{\ldots x_0\})$;

(4) $SIN|SC(A = \{x_0 \ldots\})$ is a subset of $SIN|SC(A)$;

(5) $SOPH|SA(A = \{\ldots x_0\})$ coincides with $B(A{:}x_0)$;

(6) $SOPH|FB(A = \{x_0 \ldots\}) = \{x_0\}$ if x_0 is the Condorcet winner in A and only if $x_0 P x_m$ and is a subset of $UC(x_0)$ in A otherwise;

(7) $SOPH|SQ(A = \{\ldots x_0\}) = \{x_0\}$ if and only if x_0 is the Condorcet winner in A and coincides with $TC(A - \{x_0\})$ otherwise; and

(8) $SOPH|SC(A = \{x_0 \ldots\})$ coincides with $SIN|SA(A = \{\ldots x_0\})$.

With respect to (1), by straightforward modification of Proposition 8, an alternative in $A - \{x_0\}$ can be brought to the final vote if and only if it belongs to $TC(A - \{x_0\})$; every such alternative that beats x_0 can be the outcome and, if some such alternative fails to beat x_0, x_0 can also. With respect to (2), let alternatives not in the path be at the beginning of the voting order (and be defeated by x_0) and let the remainder of the voting order follow the reverse of the path. With respect to (3), by a straightforward modification of Proposition 4, every alternative in $TC(A - \{x_0\})$ can be brought to the final vote and those that beat x_0 can be the outcome (but it may be that other alternatives can be brought to the final vote and beat x_0 also). With respect to (4), x_0 is the outcome if and only if it is the majority winner, and a necessary condition for an alternative in $A - \{x_0\}$ to be the outcome is that it beat at least one other alternative in A other than x_0. Point (5) follows directly from the sophisticated equivalent agenda for amendment procedure. (Recall that $B(A{:}x_0)$ is the subset of $B(A)$ made up of top elements of all Banks chains with bottom element x_0.) Similarly, with respect to point (6), if x_m beats x_0, consider any alternative x covered in A by x_0; no chain in A with top element x can be a Banks chain, because x_0 can be placed on top of it. Points (7) and (8) likewise follow from the sophisticated equivalent agenda for successive/sequential procedure, together with the fact the x_0 is last in the voting order under sequential procedure and first under successive procedure.

Variable Agenda Set and Voting Order   Now let us suppose that the agenda setter can choose the subset of alternatives in X that belong to the agenda set A, subject to the constraint that A must include the status quo x_0. Again we ask what alternatives are possible sincere or sophisticated voting outcomes under various procedures. For convenience, we suppose that the agenda setter has 'gatekeeping' power in that he can refrain from making any proposal, so x_0 is always a possible outcome (even if x_0 is the Condorcet loser in X). For the moment, we suppose that x_0, though it must appear on the agenda, can be placed anywhere in the voting order. We let $SIN(X:x_0 \in A)$ and $SOPH(X:x_0 \in A)$ designate the sets of alternatives in X that can be the sincere and sophisticated voting outcomes respectively, given that the agenda must include x_0 somewhere in the voting order. (Since the voting order is unconstrained, there is no distinction between sequential or successive agendas or between backward- or forward-built amendment agendas.) Proposition 26 demarcates or bounds these sets.

PROPOSITION 26: *If any agenda set A may be formed out of X, subject to the constraint that x_0 belongs to A:*

(1) $SIN|S(X:x_0 \in A)$ is a superset of $\bar{\mathcal{P}}(x_0)$;
(2) $SIN|A(X:x_0 \in A)$ coincides with $\bar{\mathcal{P}}(x_0)$;
(3) $SOPH|S(X:x_0 \in A)$ coincides with $\bar{\mathcal{P}}(x_0)$; and
(4) $SOPH|A(X:x_0 \in A)$ coincides with $UC(x_0)$.

With respect to (1) and (2), suppose x (distinct from x_0) belongs to $\bar{\mathcal{P}}(x_0)$; by definition there is a sequence of alternatives such that $xP \ldots Px_0$. We then can design a successive or amendment agenda including just these alternatives with the voting order the reverse of the sequence. By the respective sincere equivalent agendas, x is the outcome in each case and, by the argument supporting Proposition 7, the condition is necessary as well as sufficient in the latter case. Point (3) follows from (2), in conjunction with the reversibility property. Point (4) was first demonstrated by Shepsle and Weingast (1984a). Suppose x belongs to $UC(x_0)$. Then either x beats x_0 or there is some z such that $xPzPx_0$. If the former, x is the outcome from the agenda $A = \{x, x_0\}$; if the latter, x is the outcome from the amendment agenda $A = \{x, x_0, z\}$ with z voted on last (so the required agenda never need include more than three alternatives). Suppose x is covered by x_0 in X; x is also covered by x_0 in any subset A that includes both x and x_0, so x does not belong to $UC(A)$. By Proposition 16, the sophisticated outcome from A belongs to $B(A)$ a subset of $UC(A)$, so x cannot be the outcome.

It is useful to interpret Proposition 26 in the case in which the alternative set X is a space of two or more dimensions and voters have standard spatial preferences. McKelvey's Global Cycling Theorem implies that $\bar{\mathcal{P}}(x) = X$

for any x in X, so agenda control is complete if voting is sincere or if successive procedure is in use.[66] (This is essentially the McKelvey model discussed in 7.1.) On the other hand, $UC(x_0)$ is bounded, so if voting is sophisticated and an amendment agenda must be used, agenda control is less than total. Recall from 5.3 that, if preferences are Euclidean and x_0 is at a distance d from the center of the yolk, $UC(x_0)$ is bounded by the circle centered on the center of the yolk with a radius of $d + 4r$, where r is the radius of the yolk, so the agenda setter can design an agenda that yields a sophisticated voting outcome at most $4r$ further away from the center of the yolk than x_0 is.[67]

Variable Agenda Set with the Position of Status Quo in the Voting Order Fixed   While Proposition 26 requires an agenda that includes x_0, it allows x_0 to appear anywhere in the voting order. We now consider the scope of the agenda setter's control over sincere and sophisticated voting outcomes when he is constrained to use a standard amendment or sequential agenda that puts x_0 last or a successive or forward-built amendment agenda that puts x_0 first. We let $SIN(X:A = \{\ldots x_0\})$ (or $SIN(X:A = \{x_0 \ldots \})$) designate the sets of alternatives in X that can be the sincere voting outcomes, given that the agenda must include x_0 last (or first) in the voting order, and likewise for sophisticated outcomes. Obviously each such set is a subset of the corresponding set $SIN(X:x_0 \in A)$ or $SOPH(X:x_0 \in A)$. Propositions 27 and 28 demarcate these sets.

PROPOSITION 27: *If any agenda set A may be chosen out of X, under backward-built agendas each set $S(X:A = \{\ldots x_0\})$ coincides with $\bar{P}(x_0)$.*

If the agenda setter makes any proposal(s), the final vote will be between x_0 and some other alternative and, since even sophisticated voters vote make sincere choice at the final vote, the voting outcome cannot lie outside of $\bar{P}(x_0)$. Moreover, any alternative x in $P(x_0)$ can be the outcome, given the agenda $A = \{x, x_0\}$.

PROPOSITION 28: *If any agenda set A may be chosen out of X, under*

[66] However, as Feld, Grofman, and Miller (1989) note, exercise of such total agenda control may require an impracticably large agenda.

[67] The scope of the setter's control thus depends on how centrally located x_0 is and on the size of the yolk. The latter parameter also determines the size of the agendas required to implement total agenda control in the preceding cases (Feld, Grofman, and Miller, 1989).

forward-built agendas:

    (1) $SIN|SC(X:A = \{x_0 \ldots \})$ coincides with $SIN|SC(X:x_0 \in A)$;

    (2) $SIN|FB(X:A = \{x_0 \ldots \})$ coincides with $\bar{P}(x_0)$;

    (3) $SOPH|SC(X:A = \{x_0 \ldots \})$ coincides with $\bar{P}(x_0)$; and

    (4) $SOPH|FB(X:A = \{x_0 \ldots \})$ coincides with $UC(x_0)$.

The arguments supporting the corresponding parts of Proposition 26 apply here as well, since the earlier arguments either permitted or required putting x_0 first in the voting order in the agenda set A.

In the context of an alternative space of two or more dimensions, point (2) corresponds to the basic McKelvey model discussed in 7.1. Point (3) indicates how the McKelvey result extends to sophisticated voting if a successive agenda is permitted.

7.3. Manipulation By Agenda Expansion

It is commonly recognized that the outcome of an election can be affected by the entry of an additional candidate, even if the new candidate does not himself win. Further, the possibility of such manipulation is generally thought to be especially great if voting is sincere and to be attenuated if voting is strategic (or 'tactical'). Under plurality voting and similar aggregation procedures, such electoral manipulation results from the reallocation of first (or other higher level) preferences among the candidates as the field expands and thus can occur even if majority preference is fully transitive.

Here we consider a similar phenomenon in the context of parliamentary voting. We set things up in this way. An agenda $A = \{x_0, x_1, \ldots , x_m\}$ has been formed, where the subscripts continue to indicate the order in which alternatives have been placed on the agenda. The agenda is of a specified type, and voting may be either sincere or sophisticated. We let x' designate the (sincere or sophisticated) voting outcome from A.

Given either sincere or sophisticated voting, we consider the consequences of *agenda expansion* resulting from the addition of some alternative x_{m+1} to the agenda, where x_{m+1} is placed into the voting order in the manner prescribed by the procedure in use. Let x'' designate the outcome from the expanded agenda A'. Such agenda expansion may have three possible consequences: (1) the voting outcome is unchanged, so that $x'' = x'$; (2) the outcome changes from x' to the newly proposed alternative, so that

$x'' = x_{m+1}$; or (3) the outcome changes from x'' to some other alternative previously on the agenda, so that $x'' \neq x'$ and $x'' \neq x_{m+1}$. If (3) can result for some x_{m+1}, we say the agenda A is *manipulable*, as a committee member with the power to expand the agenda may have an incentive to manipulate the voting outcome by adding an alternative that nevertheless will not be the voting outcome. If an agenda is manipulable, the *scope of manipulation* is the subset of alternatives in A, identified in terms of their place in the voting order, that can possibly be made the voting outcome as a result of agenda expansion. (This subset is always a string of adjacent alternatives in the voting order; which one becomes the actual outcome depends on voter preferences.) Conversely, if (3) cannot result (regardless of what agenda A has initially been formed and regardless of what alternative x_{m+1} in $X - A$ is newly proposed), we say an agenda is *immune to manipulation*.[68] If, for a particular agenda A and any possible new proposal x_{m+1}, only (1) can result, we say A is *invulnerable to expansion*.

We consider these questions for both sincere and sophisticated voting under various types of agendas that entail definite voting orders. The results are summarized in the following propositions, which are essentially self-evident once stated.

We first consider expansion of a sequential agenda, given sincere voting. The new proposal x_{m+1} thus becomes the *first* alternative in the voting order $m_{x+1}, x_m, \ldots, x_0$. If the new proposal x_{m+1} is the majority winner in A', every element of the sincere equivalent agenda is equal to x_{m+1}; otherwise, the sincere equivalent agenda is unchanged except for the additional element x_{m+1} at the outset.

PROPOSITION 29: *Given sincere voting under a sequential agenda:*

(1) $x'' = x_{m+1}$ if and only if x_{m+1} in the majority winner in A';

(2) $x'' = x'$ otherwise; so

(3)   the agenda is immune to manipulation; and

(4) A is invulnerable to expansion if and only if there is no z in $X - A$ such that z is the majority winner in $A \cup \{z\}$.

We may observe that (4) is an 'easy' condition to meet, especially if the agenda A is already fairly large.

---

[68] Put otherwise, voting from an agenda that is immune from manipulation obeys the weak axiom of revealed preference.

We next consider expansion of a successive agenda, given sincere voting. The new proposal x_{m+1} thus becomes the *last* alternative in the voting order $x_0, \ldots, x_m, x_{m+1}$. We note that if x_k fails to be a majority winner in $\{x_k, \ldots, x_m\}$, x_k certainly fails to be a majority winner in $\{x_k, \ldots, x_m, x_{m+1}\}$.

PROPOSITION 30: *Given sincere voting under a successive agenda:*

   (1) $x'' = x_{m+1}$ *if* x_{m+1} *is a Condorcet winner in* A' *and only if* $x_{m+1} P x_m$;

   (2) *if* $x'' \neq x'$, x'' *follows* x' *in the voting order, so the scope of manipulation is* $\{x_{k+1}, \ldots, x_m\}$, *where* $x_k = x'$; *so*

   (3) *the agenda is immune to manipulation if* $x' = x_m$; *and*

   (4) *A is invulnerable to expansion if there is no z in* $X - A$ *such that* $x' = x_k$ *fails to be the majority winner in* $\{x_k, \ldots x_m, z\}$.

We next consider expansion of a standard (backward-built) amendment agenda, given sincere voting. The new alternative x_{m+1} thus becomes the *first* alternative in the voting order $x_{m+1}, x_m, \ldots, x_0$. We note that if the x_{m+1} cannot beat x_m, the sincere equivalent agenda is unchanged, except for the additional element x_{m+1} at the outset.

PROPOSITION 31: *Given sincere voting under a standard amendment agent:*

   (1) $x'' = x_{m+1}$ *if and only if* x_{m+1} *is the Condorcet winner in* A';

   (2) $x'' = x'$ *if* $x_m P x_{m+1}$ *or if* x' *is the Condorcet winner in* A';

   (3) *if* $x_{m+1} P x_m$ *but* x_{m+1} *is not the Condorcet winner in* A', *the agenda A is manipulable;*

   (4) *if A is manipulable, the scope of manipulation is maximal, i.e.,* $\{x_m, \ldots x_0\}$; *and*

   (5) *A is invulnerable to expansion if* x' *is the Condorcet winner in* X *or if* $x_m P z$ *for all* z *in* $X - A$.

If an amendment agenda is forward-built, the new alternative x_{m+1} becomes the *last* alternative in the voting order $x_0, \ldots, x_m, x_{m+1}$. The sincere equivalent agenda $(d_0, \ldots, d_m)$ is unchanged, except that a new element d_{m+1} is added at the end, where $d_{m+1} = d_m$ if $d_m P x_{m+1}$ and $d_{m+1} = x_{m+1}$ if $x_{m+1} P d_m$.

PROPOSITION 32: *Given sincere voting under a forward-built amendment agenda:*

(1) $x'' = x_{m+1}$ if and only if $x_{m+1} P x'$;

(2) $x'' = x'$ otherwise.

(3) the agenda is immune to manipulation; and

(4) A is invulnerable to expansion if and only if $x' P z$ for all z in $X - A$.

Finally, with respect to sincere voting, we consider this situation: a standard amendment agenda has been formed and a new alternative x_{m+1} is proposed *as a substitute bill.* This results in a (degenerate) two-stage amendment agenda with $A^2 = \{x_{m+1}\}$, equivalent to a (one-stage) amendment agenda with voting order $x_m, \ldots, x_1, x_{m+1}, x_0$. Let x^1 designate the preliminary outcome from A^1. Thus $x' = x^1$ if $x^1 P x_0$ and $x' = x_0$ otherwise.

PROPOSITION 33: *Given sincere voting under a standard amendment agenda, where x_{m+1} is a substitute:*

(1) $x'' = x_{m+1}$ if and only if $x_{m+1} P x^1$ and $x_{m+1} P x_0$;

(2) the agenda is manipulable if and only if $x^1 P x_0 P x_{m+1} P x^1$; so

(3) the scope of agenda manipulation is minimal, i.e., $\{x_0\}$;

(4) A is invulnerable to expansion (via a substitute proposal) if and only if $\{x', x_0\}$ is externally stable in $X - A$.

We now turn to sophisticated voting. By the reversibility principle, the analysis for sophisticated voting under a sequential agenda is identical to that for sincere voting under a forward-built amendment agenda.

PROPOSITION 34: *Given sophisticated voting under a sequential agenda:*

(1) $x'' = x_{m+1}$ if and only if $x_{m+1} P x'$;

(2) $x'' = x'$ otherwise; so

(3) the agenda is immune to manipulation; and

(4) A is invulnerable to expansion if $x' P z$ for all z in $X - A$.

By the same reversibility principle, the analysis of sophisticated voting under a successive agenda is identical to that for sincere voting under a standard (backward-built) amendment agenda.

PROPOSITION 35: *Given sophisticated voting under a successive agenda:*

(1) $x'' = x_{m+1}$ *if and only if* x_{m+1} *is the Condorcet winner in* A';

(2) $x'' = x'$ *if* $x_m P x_{m+1}$ *or if* x' *is the Condorcet winner in* A';

(3)   *if* $x_{m+1} P x_m$ *but* x_{m+1} *is not the Condorcet winner in* A', *the agenda A is manipulable;*

(4)   *if A is manipulable, the scope of manipulation is maximal, i.e.,* $\{x_m, \ldots, x_0\}$; *and*

(5)   *A is invulnerable to expansion if* x' *is the Condorcet winner in X or if* $x_m P z$ *for all z in* $X - A$.

We now consider expansion of a standard (backward-built) amendment agenda, given sophisticated voting. The analysis follows directly from consideration of the Banks chain entailed by the sophisticated equivalent agenda (noted in connection with Proposition 16).

PROPOSITION 36: *Given sophisticated voting under a standard (backward-built) amendment agenda:*

(1) $x'' = x_{m+1}$ *if and only if* x_{m+1} *can be placed on top of the chain* $< z_k, \ldots, z_0 >$, *where* $z_k = x'$;

(2) $x'' = x'$ *otherwise; so*

(3)   *the agenda is immune to manipulation; and*

(4)   *A is invulnerable to expansion if and only if the chain* $< x_k, \ldots, x_0 >$, *where* $x_k = x'$, *is externally stable in X.*

We now consider expansion of a forward-built amendment agenda, given sophisticated voting. We note that if $x_m P x_{m+1}$, the sophisticated equivalent agenda is unchanged except for the additional element at the end, but otherwise the equivalent agenda may be totally changed.

PROPOSITION 37: *Given sophisticated voting under a forward-built amendment agenda:*

(1) $x'' = x_{m+1}$ *if and only if* x_{m+1} *is the Condorcet winner in* A';

(2) $x'' = x'$ *if* $x_m P x_{m+1}$;

(3)   *otherwise the agenda is manipulable, and the scope of manipulation is almost maximal, i.e.,* $\{x_0, \ldots, x_{m-1}\}$; *and*

(4)   A is invulnerable to expansion if x' is the Condorcet winner in X or if $x_m P z$ for all z in $X - A$.

Finally, we consider the expansion of a standard amendment agenda resulting from a proposed substitute, when voting is sophisticated.

PROPOSITION 38: *Given sophisticated voting under a standard amendment agenda, where x_{m+1} is a substitute:*

(1) $x'' = x_0$ only if $x' = x_0$ (i.e., only if x_0 is the Condorcet winner in A);

(2) $x'' = x'$ if $x_0 P x_{m+1}$;

(3) $x'' = x_{m+1}$ if and only if $x_{m+1} P x_0$ and $\{x_{m+1}, x_0\}$ is externally stable in A';

(4)   the agenda is manipulable only if $\{x_{m+1}, x_0\}$ fails to be externally stable in A';

(5)   the scope of agenda manipulation is almost maximal, i.e., $\{x_m, \dots, x_1\}$; and

(6)   A is invulnerable expansion (via a substitute proposal) if, for every z in $X - A$, $x_0 P z$ or $\{z, x_0\}$ is externally stable in X.

We may note several things in conclusion. First, while agenda manipulation under sequential binary procedure clearly can occur, several types of binary agendas are immune to manipulation given either sincere or sophisticated voting. In fact, sequential agendas are immune to manipulation given both types of voting. We may also note that voter sophistication does not necessarily reduce the possibility or scope of agenda manipulation, except in the very important case of standard amendment agendas. For all other types of agendas we have examined, sophistication either makes manipulation possible where it is not under sincerity, increases the scope of manipulation, or makes no difference.

Finally, in so far as agenda manipulation can occur under any voting process dependent only on the majority preference tournament, it is due entirely to intransitivities in majority preference. Thus, if majority preference is transitive (e.g., if voter preferences are single-peaked), every pairwise agenda is immune to manipulation (regardless of whether voting is sincere or sophisticated) and every sequential binary agenda is immune to manipulation if voting is sophisticated. In each case specified, x' is the Condorcet winner in A and x'' is the Condorcet winner in A', so x'' is either x_{m+1} or x'.

8. AGENDA FORMATION

In the previous section, we examined the extent to which an agenda setter
could control voting outcomes. But we did not consider the motivation of
the agenda setter and how he might exercise this control in the service of
his preferences. In this final section, we consider how a monopoly agenda
setter, a 'gatekeeping' agenda setter, and competing agenda setters might
exploit their control. We also consider how an 'open' agenda formation
process might work. In each case, we try to identify sincere and (especially)
sophisticated outcomes of the overall process of agenda formation and
voting.

In considering agenda formation, we are in effect placing one or more
'agenda setting moves' on top of the agenda tree. Typically, these moves
are not binary — an agenda setter is likely to have a multiplicity of choices.
On the other hand, unlike the decision nodes of the agenda tree itself, these
moves are uniquely assigned to a particular voter — that is, to an agenda
setter. Moreover, if there is a sequence of such moves assigned to different
agenda setters, we may reasonably assume that the setter who exercises a later
move knows what a setter assigned an earlier move has done. This implies
that we can extend the backwards induction logic underlying the analysis
of sophisticated voting up to the top of the extended tree that incorporates
agenda setting moves, and we can thereby identify the sophisticated outcome
of the entire process. (Of course, determination of sophisticated equivalents
at the agenda-formation nodes depends not on the collective preferences of
all voters but on the individual preferences of the voter assigned the particular
agenda-setting move.)

Like an ordinary voter, an agenda setter may behave in either a sincere or
sophisticated fashion. And given two (or more) agenda setters, we need to
consider whether there is an incentive for them to collude. A *sincere agenda
setter* always proposes his most preferred alternative in X. A *sophisticated
agenda setter* makes his proposal on the basis of the anticipated final voting
outcome.[69] If he has monopoly agenda power (or if he is making the final
move in a competitive agenda-setting game), the sophisticated setter can

---

[69] This distinction was introduced independently by Denzau and Mackay (1983) and
Krehbiel (1985 and 1987), in both cases to modify Shepsle's (1979) notion of 'structure-
induced equilibrium' in a legislative setting. In these works (which belong to the 'institutional'
literature referred to in footnote 1), the 'agenda setter' is itself a committee (modelled on a
U.S. Congressional Committee), whose plural membership may have diverse preferences. A
sincere committee is one whose internal voting is sincere (or whose sophistication, if any, is

calculate the voting outcome of every agenda he might design (or complete) and make his proposal accordingly; if he is making an earlier move in a competitive agenda setting game, he can anticipate the optimal response of the other setter and the resulting voting outcome for each proposal he might make and makes his proposal accordingly. *Collusive agenda setters* negotiate a final outcome between themselves and then design an agenda that will induce voters to ratify it.

A further question is whether, after the agenda has been fixed, subsequent voting behavior is sincere or sophisticated (or cooperative) and what agenda setters expect in this regard. The behavior of sincere agenda setters is not conditioned on this expectation but that of sophisticated setters may be. Often, however, agendas resulting from agenda-setting games are sufficiently small and simple that the final outcome does not depend on the particular type of voting behavior.

Throughout this section we assume that the status quo x_0 is *not* the Condorcet winner in X, for otherwise questions of agenda formation become trivial.

8.1. Monopoly Agenda Formation

Suppose we have a set X of alternatives and a set N of voters with preferences over all alternatives in X. There is a single distinguished committee member i, the *monopoly agenda setter*, who has the right to form the agenda set A, subject to the constraint that A must include the status quo x_0. We assume the agenda structure is of the standard amendment type with x_0 voted on last.[70]

Let us consider the following example, which shows a majority preference tournament over a set X of alternatives (including a status quo x_0) and selected preference orderings with which an agenda setter may be endowed.

---

oriented only toward the committee proposal); a sophisticated committee is one whose internal voting is oriented toward the final 'floor' outcome. Other works, e.g., Niskanen (1971), Romer and Rosenthal (1978 and 1979), and Mackay and Weaver (1983), interpret an agenda setter as a (unitary) bureaucrat or agency making a proposal to a legislature or to an electorate (for referendum); for a survey, see Rosenthal (1990). In such analyses, it may be plausible to suppose that information is incomplete and that the agenda setter is better informed than the voters. But this takes us beyond the scope of the present survey; see Banks (1990 and 1993) and also Banks (1991: pp. 27ff) in this series and the literature cited therein.

[70] We make this assumption for ease of exposition. As noted in several footnotes, it can be relaxed, using appropriate Propositions from Section 7.

EXAMPLE 14

Majority Preference Tournament

R^1	R^2	R^3	R^4
w	a	v	a
v	y	a	x_0
a	x_0	x_0	z
x_0	w	z	v
y	z	y	y
z	v	w	w

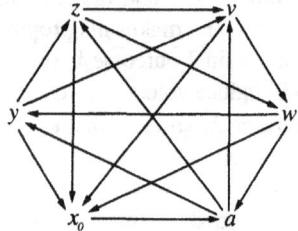

If the monopoly agenda setter is *sincere*, he proposes his most preferred alternative x^{i^*} in X, forming the agenda set $A = \{x^{i^*}, x_0\}$ and makes no proposal if he happens to most prefer x_0, so (regardless of the type of voting behavior) the final outcome is x^{i^*} if and only if $x^{i^*} P x_0$ and is x_0 otherwise; in any event, the outcome belongs to $\bar{P}(x_0)$. Thus, if the setter has ordering R^1, he proposes w, which becomes the outcome; if he has ordering R^3, he proposes v, which becomes the outcome; if he has orderings R^2 or R^4, he proposes a and the outcome is x_0. (In Example 14, $\bar{P}(x_0) = \{y, z, v, w, x_0\}$ so a, despite its strength in majority preference, cannot be the outcome.)

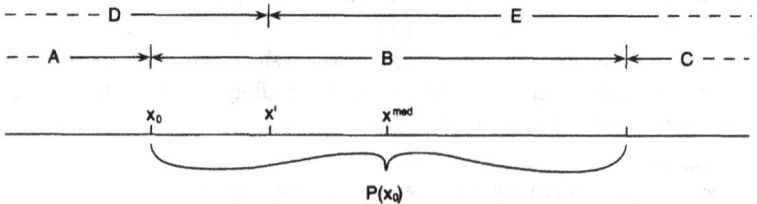

FIGURE 16   Agenda Setting in One Dimension

Likewise, we may consider the one-dimensional alternative space shown in Figure 16, over which both voters and the agenda setter have single-peaked preferences. Figure 16 shows the status quo alternative x_0, the

Condorcet winner x^{med}, and the interval $P(x_0)$.[71] If the sincere agenda setter's ideal point x^{i^*} lies in $P(x_0)$, the outcome is x^{i^*}; otherwise, the outcome is x_0.

Let us now suppose the agenda setter is sophisticated. For each agenda that he might form, there is a determinate voting outcome that the agenda setter (knowing voter preferences and behavior) can anticipate. Thus in choosing from among possible agendas, he is — in effect and with full knowledge — choosing from among possible voting outcomes. Whether voting is sincere or sophisticated, we — and the agenda setter — know (from Proposition 27) that, given x_0 is voted on last, the voting outcome must belong to $\bar{P}(x_0)$. If there is no alternative in $P(x_0)$ that the setter prefers to x_0, he may as well make no proposal. Otherwise, the agenda setter can do no better than propose a single alternative x in $P(x_0)$ for, if there is some larger agenda that yields x as the voting outcome, both the sincere and sophisticated equivalent agendas for amendment procedure imply that $x P x_0$, so the agenda set $A = \{x, x_0\}$ yields the same outcome. Thus a sophisticated monopoly agenda setter is not ultimately concerned whether voting is sincere or sophisticated, can confine his attention to two-element agendas, and need only identify the single alternative to place on the agenda with the status quo. The sophisticated agenda setter i therefore proposes the agenda $\{x, x_0\}$, where $\{x\} = C_i[P(x_0) \cap P_i(x_0)]$. If the intersection is empty, he makes no proposal and the status quo is maintained.[72]

Consider again the setter preferences shown in Example 14. Given the preference ordering R^1 or R^3, sophisticated agenda setting behavior is the same as sincere; but given R^2, i proposes y, which becomes the voting outcome, and given R^4, i makes no proposal and the status quo x_0 is maintained. Given the configuration in Figure 16, the agenda setter makes a proposal and the status quo is changed provided his ideal point x^{i^*} lies on the same side of x_0 as x^{med} does. In general, a proposal is more likely to be forthcoming from a sincere agenda setter; at the same time, the status quo is more likely to be changed given a sophisticated agenda setter.

---

[71] If preferences are symmetric single-peaked, x^{med} is at the midpoint of this interval; it is in interior of the interval in any event.

[72] By Proposition 27, the setter's calculations would be the same even if he were allowed to form any backwards-built agenda but, by Proposition 28, he would have considerably more room for maneuver if he could form a forward-built agenda.

It is evident that, given a monopoly agenda setter, the final voting outcome is determined mostly by the setter's preferences and is only somewhat constrained by voter preferences. Specifically, voter preferences make a difference only with respect to the manner in which they partition the set of alternatives other than the status quo into the two sets $P(x_0)$ and $P^{-1}(x_0)$. Majority preference within or between these sets has no effect on the final voting outcome.

A sophisticated monopoly agenda setter makes a proposal if and only if the intersection $P(x_0) \cap P_i(x_0)$ is non-empty, and he proposes his most preferred alternative in this intersection. This leads to two clear and essentially intuitive implications. One relates to the first element in the intersection: the 'power' of the agenda setter depends on the degree of unpopularity of the status quo. If there are many alternatives that beat the status quo, the setter can make many non-innocuous proposals; if there are only a few alternatives that beat the status quo, he can make only a few non-innocuous proposals (and if the status quo is the Condorcet winner, he can make no non-innocuous proposal). This is most clearly illustrated by the spatial example in Figure 16. If x_0 is close to x^{med}, $P(x_0)$ is small; if x_0 is far from the median, $P(x_0)$ is large.

The other implication follows from the scope of the intersection $P(x_0) \cap P_i(x_0)$ itself. However great his 'power,' the agenda setter benefits from it only to the extent that his preferences are congruent with majority preferences *vis à vis* the status quo. In Figure 16, if the agenda setter's ideal point x^{i*} lies on the opposite side of x_0 from x^{med} (region A), he cannot benefit from his agenda power at all; if x^{i*} lies within $P(x_0)$ (region B), he can benefit maximally from his power and achieve his ideal; if x^{i*} lies beyond the boundary of $P(x_0)$ opposite x_0 (region C), he can benefit considerably from his power but cannot attain his ideal.[73]

---

[73] Thus a monopoly agenda setter with relatively extreme preferences would try to establish a status quo (or reversion level) that is extreme in the opposite direction. This argument is developed, together with empirical analysis pertaining to school budget referenda, by Romer and Rosenthal (1978 and 1979). The spatial case presents a mathematical problem in the event the setter's ideal point lies in region C in Figure 16. In this event $C_i[P(x_0)]$ is strictly undefined, since $P(x_0)$ is an 'open set' (that does not include its boundary). Essentially, the setter wants to propose an alternative as close to the right boundary of $P(x_0)$ as possible without actually being on the boundary, but for every alternative he might propose there is another one ever so slightly closer. In the real political world, an agenda setter runs risks in making a proposal very close to the (estimated) boundary of $P(x_0)$ that are independent of this mathematical problem.

8.2. Gatekeeping and Agenda Formation

An agenda setter has *gatekeeping* power if no voting occurs in the absence of a proposal from the setter, so the setter can always maintain the status quo as the outcome. A monopoly agenda setter has gatekeeping power, but a gatekeeper need not have monopoly agenda control because, in the event he does 'open the gates' by making a proposal, others may have the right to add alternatives to the agenda. Put otherwise, a gatekeeper is a monopoly agenda setter if his proposal goes to the voting body under a *closed rule* — that is, if no amendments are permitted 'from the floor' (or elsewhere); he is merely a gatekeeper, without monopoly control, if his proposal goes to the voting body under an *open rule* — that is, if amendments are permitted 'from the floor' (or elsewhere).[74]

How is the behavior of agenda setter i affected if he has merely gate keeping power, not monopoly agenda control? If he is sincere, his behavior is unchanged; by definition, he proposes his most preferred alternative x^{i^*} (unless $x^{i^*} = x_0$). But such a proposal, even if non-innocuous, may well be self-defeating, since it 'opens the gates' and may lead, via the proposal and adoption of amendments, to a final outcome that the agenda setter likes less than x_0 (which he could have secured by making no proposal). A sophisticated gatekeeper foresees this possibility and is accordingly more conservative about making a proposal. However, once the setter 'opens the gates' by proposing some alternative x^i, an open agenda formation process results, so precise foresight is not always possible. A commonly made assumption (Denzau and Mackay, 1983; Krehbiel, 1987) that may allow complete foresight is that admissible amendments are subject to a *germaneness rule* — that is, they must pertain to the same 'dimension' or 'issue' raised by the choice between x_0 and the setter's proposal x^i. In spatial terms, this is taken to mean that all amendments must lie on the straight line L that passes through x_0 and x^i, so plausibly voters have single-peaked preferences over the set L of admissible alternatives and over whatever particular agenda set A is actually formed out of L.[75] Moreover, if at any point in the agenda formation process the Condorcet winner x^* in L has

---

[74] U.S. Congressional Committees are customarily said to have gatekeeping power (subject to some limitations) with respect to their assigned jurisdictions. The terminology of open vs. closed rules derives from procedure in the U.S. House of Representatives.

[75] The U.S. House of Representatives (but not the Senate) has such a germaneness rule, though it is doubtful that this implies that all House agendas are genuinely one-dimensional.

not been proposed, some voter (indeed, a majority) has an incentive to see that it is proposed and, once it is (and given an amendment agenda), it must become the voting outcome (whether voting is sincere or sophisticated). Thus the sophisticated agenda setter i knows he has just two choices: make no proposal and sustain x_0 as the outcome, or make *any* proposal and get x^* as the outcome. Therefore, he makes a proposal — it does not matter *what* he proposes — and 'opens the gates' if and only if $x^* P_i x_0$. Let the one-dimensional space in Figure 16 now represent the set L of alternatives 'germane' to whatever proposal the gatekeeper may make. There is some point x' between x_0 and $x^{\text{med}} = x^*$ (exactly at the midpoint, if the setter's single-peaked preferences are symmetric) such that, if his ideal point lies to the right of x' (in region E), the setter makes a proposal, whereas if his ideal point lies to the left of x' (in region D), the setter makes no proposal.[76]

In the absence of unidimensionality induced by a germaneness rule, several things change. First, because there may be no Condorcet winner among the non-innocuous proposals that might be proposed, the agenda setter may not be able fully to foresee the consequences of 'opening the gates' to what subsequently becomes an open and unstructured agenda formation process (so the present discussion relates to that in 8.4). Second, if the setter chooses to 'open the gates', he must also be concerned with how he does so — *what he proposes*, not just *whether he makes a proposal*, is now relevant. Indeed, he may even chose to propose an alternative he likes less that the status quo x_0.

Let us assume the following. First, recall that we assume throughout that x_0 is not the Condorcet winner in X. Second, a backward-built amendment agenda is formed, so the status quo is last in the voting order and the setter's proposal is second-to-last. Third, committee voting is sophisticated, and the agenda setter knows this.[77]

Let $F(x)$ designate the set of alternatives that are possible voting outcomes given only that the gatekeeper proposes x (together with the assumptions noted above). It follows that $F(x) = \bar{P}(x_0)$ if and only if $x_0 R x$ (i.e., the

---

[76] Krehbiel (1985) characterizes the latter situation as 'ripe for obstruction.' Note that if the setter's ideal point lies between x_0 and x', both the setter and a majority of voters would benefit if the setter had monopoly control, for the outcome would then be the setter's ideal point, preferred by a majority of voters to x_0.

[77] We could allow other types of agendas and/or sincere voting and use the appropriate propositions from Section 7. However, analysis would be more complex and the results less clean, especially as agenda manipulation might then be possible.

setter makes an innocuous proposal), and $F(x) = P(x_0) \cap \bar{P}(x)$ otherwise (i.e., the setter makes a non-innocuous proposal).

Let $F^*(x)$ designate the set of possible voting outcomes, given that the gatekeeper proposes x and the subsequent open agenda formation reaches equilibrium, in that an agenda is formed that is invulnerable to further expansion. It follows from Proposition 36 that equilibrium is reached if and only if a sophisticated equivalent agenda has been created that is externally stable in X. From this it follows that $F^*(x) = B(X{:}x, x_0)$ if x is non-innocuous and $F^*(x) = B(X{:}x_0)$ otherwise. (Recall that $B(X{:}x_0)$ is the set of all top elements of Banks chains in X that have x_0 as bottom element; $B(X{:}x, x_0)$ is the subset of $B(X{:}x_0)$ that results when it is further specified that x is the second-to-bottom element.) Clearly, if there is a Condorcet winner x^* in $F(x)$, then $F^*(x) = \{x^*\}$, so the conclusion above for single-peaked preferences under a germaneness rule is a corollary to this conclusion.

Let us now return to Example 14. Since the number of alternatives in X is small, the gatekeeping agenda setter can in fact always exercise sufficient foresight to determine precisely what proposal to make. He can anticipate final voting outcomes as follows:

$$F^*(x_0) = \{y, z, w\}; \qquad F^*(z) = \{y\};$$
$$F^*(a) = \{y, z, w\}; \qquad F^*(v) = \{y\}; \quad \text{and}$$
$$F^*(y) = \{w\}; \qquad F^*(w) = \{z\}.$$

Note that, for each non-innocuous proposal x, $F^*(x)$ is a subset of $F^*(a)$, where a is an innocuous proposal (or x_0) and that $F^*(z)$ is the same for all such proposals. This follows necessarily from the analysis above. What is further true here, but does not hold generally, is that $F^*(x)$ is a one-element set for all non-innocuous proposals x. Thus, in this example, the setter can definitively identify his optimal proposal. Given preference orderings R^1, the setter proposes y (even though y ranks lower in his preference ordering than the status quo x_0 that he can sustain by making no proposal). Given his proposal of y, the setter can anticipate that the non-innocuous proposal of w will in due course be made from the floor (because, until it is, the agenda remains vulnerable to expansion), and then w — the setter's first preference — will become the voting outcome. If the setter were to propose w himself (or, indeed, anything he actually prefers to the status quo), the final outcome would be worse than w — indeed worse than x_0 — from his point of view. Given ordering R^2, the setter does best to propose either z or v, leading to outcome y. Given ordering R^3, the setter does best to keep the gates closed, since *any* proposal leads to an outcome inferior to x_0. Given ordering R^4, the setter clearly does best to keep the gates closed.

Given a larger finite set of alternatives, the sets $F^*(x)$ may be multi-element sets for some (or all) alternatives x, so the agenda setter will not be able fully to anticipate the outcome resulting from each proposal he might make. Given an alternative space X of two or more dimensions, this will almost always be the case. Even so, a gatekeeping agenda setter will want in general to consider not just whether to make a proposal but what to propose, since different proposals will put different constraints on the set of outcomes he can anticipate.[78]

8.3. Competitive Agenda Formation

Suppose there are two distinguished committee members i and j, each of whom has the power to put an alternative on an agenda that also includes the status quo. More specifically, the *primary agenda setter i* can propose a motion x^i, and the *secondary agenda setter j* can propose an amendment x^j to that motion.[79] In this way, a three-element agenda set $A = \{x^j, x^i, x_0\}$ is formed endogenously and voted on by the whole committee. Throughout this subsection (and the next), we assume that standard amendment procedure is employed, with the voting order established by the parliamentary status of the alternatives, so the first vote is on the amendment and the second is on the motion.

If the setters are sincere, they propose their most preferred alternatives x^{i^*} and x^{j^*}. Regardless of whether voting is sincere or sophisticated, a proposal that beats both x_0 and the other proposal is the outcome, and x_0 is the outcome if x_0 beats both proposals. If $x^{i^*} P x_0 P x^{j^*} P x^{i^*}$, x_0 is the

---

[78] Which alternative in each set would actually become the voting decision would depend on the order in which proposals were made on the floor — an essentially random matter, so far as the agenda setter can tell. The setter might evaluate these sets in terms of their worst possible outcomes and choose on a 'maximin' basis (as suggested by Banks and Gasmi, 1987, in a related context; see 8.4 below). Weingast (1989) suggests two additional considerations. First, the gatekeeping agenda setter would do well, if permitted, to make two (or even more) proposals, e.g., a motion x and an 'amendment in the nature of a substitute' x', and thereby constrain the final outcome to $B(X:x',x,x_0)$ instead of just $B(X:x,x_0)$. Second, the agenda setter can benefit by 'fighting fire with fire,' i.e., proposing counter-amendments as amendments are offered from the floor.

[79] In the U.S. Congressional context, the primary setter might be the leadership of the majority party and the secondary setter might be the leadership of the minority party (where, however, party discipline does not hold on the floor).

outcome if voting is sincere and x^{i^*} is the outcome if voting is sophisticated; and if $x^{j^*} P x_0 P x^{i^*} P x^{j^*}$, x_0 is the outcome if voting is sincere and x^{j^*} is the outcome if voting is sophisticated. In any event, it makes no difference which setter is primary and which secondary.

Henceforth, we assume sophisticated behavior on the part of all participants (which implies that the agenda setters know each other's, as well as voters', preferences). It is clear this agenda setting game leads to a determinate outcome, which can be calculated in any particular case by carrying the backwards induction back through the two agenda setting moves.[80]

The primary agenda setter i exercises his move by proposing an alternative x^i in X. (For i to propose the status quo, so that $x^i = x_0$, is equivalent to i's making no proposal.) Then the secondary agenda setter j, knowing what i has done, likewise exercises his move by proposing an alternative x^j in X. (For j to propose the status quo or match i's proposal, so that $x^j = x_0$ or $x^j = x^i$, is equivalent to j's making no proposal.) We suppose that i does not have gatekeeping power, so j can make a proposal regardless of whether or not i does. The result of these two agenda setting moves is the endogenous formation of an agenda $A = \{x^j, x^i, x_0\}$, on which the committee votes in a sophisticated fashion under standard amendment procedure.

Let $D(x)$ be the set of possible sophisticated voting outcomes in the event the primary setter proposes x. It follows that $D(x) = \bar{P}(x) \cap P(x_0)$ if x is non-innocuous and $D(x) = \bar{P}(x_0)$ otherwise. If the secondary setter

---

[80] Such agenda setting results in a 'Stackelberg game' in which i is the leader and j the follower. For similar formulations, see Banks and Gasmi (1987) and Weingast (1989); in so far as it focuses on the discrete alternative case, the following discussion builds in part on Miller (1986). One variant of competitive agenda setting is well established in voting theory, namely the model of *electoral competition*, in which the agenda setters are *political parties* (or *candidates*), each of whom selects a *policy package* or *platform* from out of a larger alternative space to put before a mass electorate, which then chooses between them. (Such a model was first explicitly formulated by Downs (1957) and was fully formalized by Davis and Hinich (1966), with many subsequent embellishments.) Most theories of electoral competition assume that parties are *power motivated* — that is, motivated solely by the desire to have their proposal win the election. In the present context, it is more plausible to assume that the setters are *policy motivated* — that is, motivated solely by the desire to see their preference over alternatives realized in the outcome. Some research on electoral competition does allow for policy motivated parties; see Calvert (1985) and references therein. Most theories of electoral competition treats parties symmetrically, in that they make their proposals simultaneously. The differentiation between primary and secondary setter here might be interpreted in electoral terms as reflecting the asymmetry between the *incumbent* and *challenger* party in a (two-party) election. (In the electoral case, there is no special status quo, so the competition is over the whole set X, rather than over $\bar{P}(x_0)$.)

proposes a (non-innocuous) alternative z in $D(x)$, z will be the final outcome; if j proposes an (innocuous) alternative z not in $D(x)$, the final outcome will be either x (if x is non-innocuous) or x_0 (otherwise), both elements of $D(x)$. Thus a sophisticated secondary agenda setter j can do no better than propose his most preferred alternative in $D(x)$, i.e., $C_j[D(x)]$, which will be the final outcome.

When primary agenda setter i makes his proposal, he can anticipate, for each proposal he might make, both j's counter-proposal and the final sophisticated voting outcome from the resulting three-element agenda. In this way, the primary setter i can deduce a mapping f_i that takes each alternative x he might propose into a final voting outcome $f_i(x)$. We have seen that $f_i(x) = C_j[D(x)]$. Let $F_i(X)$ be the collection of all alternatives z such that $z = f_i(x)$ for some x — that is, $F_i(X)$ is the subset of alternatives that primary setter i can bring about as the final voting outcome, given sophisticated behavior by the secondary setter and the voters. Thus the primary setter i aims to bring about the voting outcome z such that z is his most preferred alternative in $F_i(X)$, i.e., $\{z\} = C_i[F_i(X)]$, and he does this by proposing some alternative x such that $f_i(x) = z$, and the final voting outcome is z. We designate the final voting outcome, when setter i is primary, as $f_i^*(X)$, and we see that $f_i^*(X) = C_i[F_i(X)]$.

Though it may seem complex, this analysis is essentially straightforward and may be illustrated with reference to Example 14. Suppose setter 1 has preference ordering R^1 and setter 2 has ordering R^2. The mappings f_1 and f_2 are as follows:

x	$D(x)$	$f_1(x)$	$f_2(x)$
y	$\{y, w\}$	y	w
z	$\{y, z\}$	y	y
v	$\{y, z, v\}$	y	v
w	$\{z, v, w\}$	w	w
a	$\{y, z, v, w, x_0\}$	y	w
x_0	$\{y, z, v, w, x_0\}$	y	w

Therefore $F_1(X) = \{y, w\}$ and $C_1[F_1(X)] = f_1^*(X) = w$, where $f_1(w) = w$; and $F_2(X) = \{y, v, w\}$ and $C_2[F_2(X)] = f_2^*(X) = y$, where $f_2(z) = y$. Thus, if 1 is the primary setter, he proposes w and 2 makes no proposal (or an innocuous one), so w is the voting outcome; and if 2 is the primary setter, he proposes z, which induces 1 to propose y, which becomes the voting outcome.

We can see that it is relatively straightforward to analyze any particular competitive agenda setting game of this sort. What is more difficult is to arrive at any general characterizations of the agenda setting process and the resulting voting outcomes. To illustrate, the final outcome in the example above differs according to which agenda setter is primary, and each setter does better in the primary role. But we should not conclude this is generally true. Again considering Example 14, if the setters have ordering R^1 and R^3, it may be checked that the outcome is v regardless of who is primary; and if the setters have orderings R^1 and R^4, the outcome is y if the R^1 setter is primary and v if the R^4 setter is primary, so R^1 does better if R^4 is primary. And we need to consider not only the contest between the two setters but also the relationship between the two setters and voter majorities. Under what circumstances do setter preferences prevail, and under what circumstances do voters have more influence? If the setters most prefer the same alternative, is it the outcome regardless of voter preferences? If voter preferences are such that there is a Condorcet winner in X, will it be the final outcome, regardless of setter preferences? It is possible to provide partial answers to such questions, but they are at present less complete and definitive than those for monopoly agenda formation games or voting games with exogenous agendas.

In moving to such answers, we begin by making several general observations. First, while the outcome of the monopoly agenda formation process depends on the majority preference tournament only to the extent it partitions X into $\bar{P}(x_0)$ and $P^{-1}(x_0)$, the outcome of the competitive agenda formation game depends much more extensively on the majority preference tournament; specifically, it depends on this partition *and* — through the family of sets $D(x)$ — the entire subtournament within $P(x_0)$. (Note that the sophisticated voting outcome from any exogenous standard agenda on the whole set X depends on precisely the same portion of the tournament.) Voter preferences are likely to be especially influential to the extent they are coherent (in the sense of approaching full transitivity). In any case, we expect outcomes to be driven more by voter preferences than in the monopoly case.

At the same time, it is clear than the setters have distinctive positions in the process and that their preferences matter importantly. Indeed, the two agenda setters *jointly* have just the same 'power' that a monopoly setter has — the question is to what extent they may compete away their joint advantage. (Of course, if setters can collude by making reliable agreements between themselves, they would agree to avoid such competition.) This in turn is likely to depend on the extent to which the setters have compatible or conflicting preferences. If their preferences are sufficiently compatible, we may expect outcomes comparable to the monopoly case; if their preferences are sufficiently conflicting, we may expect outcomes much more responsive to voter preferences. Therefore, we need to be able to summarize the extent to which setter preferences are compatible or conflicting. Let us write $x P_{ij} y$ if both i and j prefer x to y.

Let $C_{ij}(X')$ be the *joint choice set* or *contract set* of i and j from some subset X' of X — that is, the set of all alternatives x in X' such that $P_{ij}(x) \cap X'$ is empty.[81] Since it represents the intersection of two orderings, the relation P_{ij} is transitive (but incomplete); it follows that for every z in X' but not in $C_{ij}(X')$, there is some x in $C_{ij}(X')$ such that $x P_{ij} z$. The most preferred alternatives in X' of i and j both belong to $C_{ij}(X')$; if and only if i and j have an identical most preferred alternative x in X', $C_{ij}(X') = \{x\}$; if and only if i and j have directly opposed orderings of the alternatives x in X', $C_{ij}(X') = X'$. Within $C_{ij}(X')$, i and j's preferences are directly opposed. ($\bar{P}(x_0)$ is the relevant subset X' of X in most of the following analysis.)

If the setters are able to collude, we expect them to agree on a pair of agenda setting strategies giving some outcome in $C_{ij}[\bar{P}(x_0)]$. If, in the absence of collusion, the final voting outcome $f^*(X)$ does not belong to $C_{ij}[\bar{P}(x_0)]$, we say the agenda setting game is *ripe for collusion* and, if collusion is possible, we expect the setters to agree on some outcome x in $C_{ij}[\bar{P}(x_0)]$ such that $x P_{ij} f^*(X)$. On the other hand, if $f^*(X)$ belongs to $C_{ij}[\bar{P}(x_0)]$, there is no room for collusive behavior between the setters.

We now make several observations concerning the mapping f. (Recall that we assume $P(x_0)$ is not empty. Note also that, if x_0 belongs to $TC(X)$, $TC[P(x_0)]$ is a proper subset of $TC(X)$; and if x does not belong to $TC(X)$, $TC[P(x_0)]$ coincides with $TC(X)$.) First, if x belongs to $TC[P(x_0)]$, $D(x)$ is contained in $TC[P(x_0)]$, so (regardless of setter preferences and regardless of which setter is primary) $f(x)$ itself belongs to $TC[P(x_0)]$; otherwise, $TC[P(x_0)]$ is contained in $D(x)$. Substantively, this implies that if the primary agenda setter proposes an alternative in $TC[P(x_0)]$, the outcome must belong to $TC[P(x_0)]$ regardless of what the secondary setter proposes. Since some x belongs to $TC[P(x_0)]$, it follows that (1) at least one element

[81] In a spatial context with standard spatial preferences, $C_{ij}(X')$ is that portion of the 'contract curve' connecting i's and j's ideal points that lies in X'.

of $F(X)$ belongs to $TC[P(x_0)]$. On the other hand, (2) if there is some v not in $TC[P(x_0)]$ such that $f(z) = v$, z cannot belong to $TC[P(x_0)]$ either; moreover (3) for any such z, $TC[P(x_0)]$ is contained in $D(z)$, so $v = f_i(z)$ implies vP_jx for all x in $TC[P(x_0)]$. Translated into substantive language: (1) the primary agenda setter can always make a proposal such that some alternative in $TC[P(x_0)]$ is the voting outcome; (2) if the primary setter can make a proposal such that some alternative v not in $TC[P(x_0)]$ is the outcome, he must propose some alternative z (which may or may not be distinct from v) also not in $TC[P(x_0)]$; and (3) the primary setter can make a proposal such that alternative v not in $TC[P(x_0)]$ is the outcome only if the secondary setter prefers v to every alternative in $TC[P(x_0)]$.

We can now derive several propositions. First we confirm our expectations in the event the setters have similar preferences.

PROPOSITION 39: *If $C_{ij}[\bar{P}(x_0)] = \{z\}$, the final voting outcome $f^*(X) = z$, regardless of voter preferences over $\bar{P}(x_0)$ and regardless of which setter is primary.*

For any x in $\bar{P}(x_0)$, x belongs to $D(x)$; therefore, if $C_{ij}[\bar{P}(x_0)] = \{z\}$, $f_i(z) = C_j[D(z)] = z$, so z belongs to $F_i(X)$ and $C_i[F_i(X)] = z$, and z is the outcome. Thus, in the extreme case in which the setters have similar preferences to the extent of sharing the same first preference from among the status quo and all alternatives that beat it, the setters will realize that preference, and voters have no more influence over the final outcome than under monopoly agenda formation.

Suppose now that setter preferences are diverse but that their contract set is confined to the top cycle of the win set of the status quo. Then the outcome is similarly confined.

PROPOSITION 40: *If $C_{ij}[P(x_0)]$ is contained in $TC[P(x_0)]$, the final voting outcome $f^*(X)$ belongs to $TC[P(x_0)]$.*

Suppose, contrary to the proposition, that the outcome is some y not in $TC[P(x_0)]$ (and, by stipulation, not in $C_{ij}[P(x_0)]$ either). We show this leads to a contradiction. Again there is some z such that $f_i(z) = y$ and z cannot belong to $TC[P(x_0)]$ either, and yP_jx for all x in $TC[P(x_0)]$. But since y — which of course must belong to $P(x_0)$ — does not belong to $C_{ij}[P(x_0)]$, there is some v such that $vP_{ij}y$ and v belongs to $C_{ij}[P(x_0)]$. But then v belongs to $TC[P(x_0)]$, so we must have both vP_jy and yP_jv.

Since $TC[P(x_0)]$ may be very large, Proposition 40 is not very helpful. What is more interesting is that, if the relationship stipulated in Proposition 40 is reversed, the implication still holds.

PROPOSITION 41: *If $TC[P(x_0)]$ is contained in $C_{ij}[P(x_0)]$, the final voting outcome $f^*(X)$ belongs to $TC[P(x_0)]$.*

Loosely, this may be interpreted as saying that if the 'top' alternatives in voter preferences all lie within the setters 'bargaining range,' the former determine where the outcome will lie within the latter.

Suppose, contrary to the proposition, that the final outcome is some y not in $TC[P(x_0)]$. Then there must be some z such that $f_i(z) = y$; as we have seen, this implies that z cannot belong to $TC[P(x_0)]$ either, and that yP_jx for all x in $TC[P(x_0)]$. But we have also seen that there is some x in $TC[P(x_0)]$ such that x also belongs to $F_i(X)$, so $y = C_i[F_i(X)]$ implies yP_ix. But then there is some x in $TC[P(x_0)]$ such that $yP_{ij}x$ and x does not belong to $C_{ij}[P(x_0)]$, contradicting the stipulation that $TC[P(x_0)$ is contained in $C_{ij}[P(x_0)]$.

This proposition has two obvious corollaries.

COROLLARY 41.1: *If the agenda setters have directly opposed preferences with respect to alternatives in $P(x_0)$, the final voting outcome $f^*(X)$ belongs to $TC[P(x_0)]$.*

Thus if setters have directly opposed interests with respect to possible outcomes, majority preference rules to the extent of constraining the outcome to $TC[P(x_0)]$, though setter preferences influence which alternative in $TC[P(x_0)]$ becomes the outcome (much as the voting order determines which alternative becomes the voting outcome given an exogenous agenda).

COROLLARY 41.2: *If there is a Condorcet winner x in $P(x_0)$ and if x belongs to $C_{ij}[P(x_0)]$, the final voting outcome $f^*(X) = x$.*

Thus if voter preferences are sufficiently coherent that there is a Condorcet winner and if setter preferences are sufficiently opposed that there is nothing they both prefer to x, voter preferences rule.

This analysis can be applied in the spatial context. Let us first consider the one-dimensional case, as shown in Figure 17. Let us suppose that the status quo x_0 is sufficiently extreme that all relevant proposals are non-innocuous, so that all points in Figure 17 belong to $P(x_0)$. The setters' contract set $C_{ij}(X)$ is the closed interval from x^{i^*} to x^{j^*}. Since majority preference is transitive and equivalent to covering, $D(x) = \bar{P}(x)$ if x is non-innocuous and $D(x) = \bar{P}(x_0)$ otherwise. There are two possible cases, depicted in Figures 17(a) and 17(b), respectively; (a) x^{i^*} and x^{j^*} 'span' x^{med}, so that x^{med}, belongs to $C_{ij}(X)$ and (b) x^{i^*} and x^{j^*} lie to the same side of x^{med}, so that x^{med} does not belong to $C_{ij}(X)$.

Consider case (a). $C_j[D(z)]$ is x^{j^*} if x^{j^*} belongs to $D(z)$; otherwise $C_j[D(z)]$ is z', where z' is the point in $D(z)$ closest to x^{j^*}.[82] In either event, for all x other than x^{med}, $f_i(x) = C_j[D(x)]$ lies on the far side of x^{med} from x^{i^*}. But $D(x^{med}) = \{x^{med}\}$ so $f(x^{med}) = x^{med}$ and $F_i(X) = x^{med}$ — that is, primary setter i should propose x^{med}, which will be the final outcome $f^*(X)$, as the agenda is invulnerable to expansion by secondary setter j. Of course, the same argument holds if j is the primary setter.

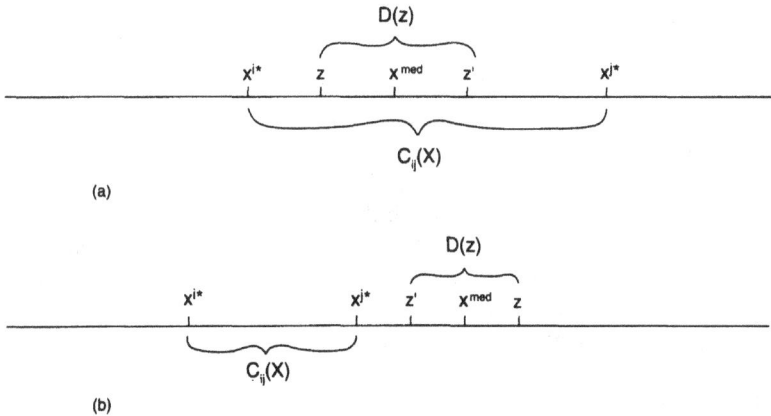

FIGURE 17 Competitive agenda setting in one dimension

---

[82] Technically, if z is on the same side of x^{med} as x^{i^*}, no such point z' exists, because $D(z)=\bar{P}(z)$ is open at the end opposite z. Substantively, j cannot propose the point on the closest boundary of $D(z)$, since this point only ties z in majority preference and — since j is proposing an amendment to i's proposal — it would lose under the standard parliamentary voting counting rule. So j must propose something just inside the boundary of $D(z)$. This is the same mathematical problem referred to in footnote 73 and it recurs at several points below.

Now consider possibility (b). This case is not symmetric with respect to the setters and their preferences: one setter is (relatively) 'extreme' (i in Figure 17(b)) and the other is (relatively) 'centrist' (j in Figure 17(b)). Let us first suppose the 'extreme' setter i is primary. As always, $C_j[D(z)]$ is x^{j^*} if x^{j^*} belongs to $D(z)$; but otherwise $C_j[D(z)]$ is z', where z' is the point in $D(z)$ closest to x^{j^*} (and x^{i^*}). In either event, for all x, $f_i(x) = C_j[D(x)]$ lies no closer to x^{i^*} than x^{j^*} does — that is, x^{j^*} is the closest point in $F_i(X)$ to x^{i^*}, so primary setter i with 'extreme' preferences can propose any x in $\bar{P}^{-1}(x^{j^*})$, to which the 'centrist' secondary setter j will respond by proposing his ideal point x^{j^*}, which will be the final outcome $f^*(X)$. If 'centrist' setter j is primary, $C_i[D(y)]$ is x^{i^*} if x^{i^*} belongs to $D(y)$; otherwise $C_j[D(z)]$ is z', where z' is the point in $D(z)$ closest to x^{i^*}. In particular, $f_j(x^{j^*}) = x^{j^*}$, so primary setter j should propose x^{j^*}, secondary setter i should make no proposal (or only an innocuous one), and again the final outcome $f^*(X)$ is x^{j^*}.

In sum, the final voting outcome $f^*(X)$ is x^{med} if x^{i^*} and x^{j^*} 'span' x^{med} and is x^{i^*} or x^{j^*}, according to which is closer to x^{med}, otherwise. In either case, the final voting outcome is independent of which setter is primary and which secondary, and there is no room for effective collusion between the agenda setters, since in any case $f^*(X)$ belongs to $C_{ij}(X)$.

We now turn to the two (or more) dimensional spatial case. We suppose all voters (including the setters) have Euclidean preferences. First we consider the admittedly special case in which there is a Condorcet winner x^*. A typical configuration of points is shown in Figure 18(a). Again we assume that the status quo x_0 is sufficiently extreme that the figure lies entirely within $P(x_0)$. The closed line segment from x^{i^*} to x^{j^*} is the setters' contract set. Considering the triangle formed by the setters' ideal points x^{i^*} and x^{j^*} and the Condorcet winner x^*, let α_i, be the angle at the x^{i^*} vertex and let α_j be the angle at the x^{j^*} vertex; the two parameters α_i and α_j characterize the configuration of three points. Let d_i and d_j be the distances from x^{i^*} and x^{j^*} respectively, to x^*. If $d_i < d_j$, we call setter i more 'moderate' and j more 'extreme' and *vice versa*. Clearly $d_i \leq d_j$ if and only if $\alpha_i \geq \alpha_j$.

Since there is a Condorcet winner, the radius of the yolk is zero, and points beat each other according to their distance from the center of the yolk (i.e., x^*). Thus, as shown in Figure 18(a), for any point x, $D(x) = \bar{P}(x)$, i.e., the area enclosed by the circle centered on x^* and passing through x (plus the point x itself), and $f_i(x)$ is the point inside this circle closest to x^{j^*} —

either x^{j^*} itself (if $\alpha_j \geq 90°$, so x^{j^*} lies inside the circle) or the intersection of the circle with the line connecting x^{j^*} and x^* (otherwise, and as shown in Figure 18(a)).[83] In like manner, $f_j(x)$ is either x^{i^*} or the intersection of the $D(x)$ circle with the line connecting x^{i^*} and x^*.

Considering all possible proposals that might be made by the primary setter, it follows that $F_i(X)$ is the closed line segment from x^{j^*} to x^* and $F_j(X)$ is the closed line segment from x^{i^*} to x^*. Thus, $f_i^*(X)$ is the point on $F_i(X)$ closest to x^{i^*}, i.e., x^{j^*} if $\alpha_j \geq 90°$, x^* if $\alpha_i + \alpha_j \leq 90°$, and the projection of x^{i^*} on the $F_i(X)$ line segment otherwise (as shown in Figure 18(b)), and likewise for $f_j^*(X)$. From this, we can readily draw several conclusions, summarized in the following proposition.

PROPOSITION 42: *In the spatial competitive agenda setting game with a Condorcet winner x^*:*

(1)   the final voting outcome is independent of which setter is primary and which secondary, i.e., $f_i^*(X) = f_j^*(X)$, if and only if $f^*(X) = x^*$, which in turn is true if and only if $\alpha_i + \alpha_j \leq 90°$;

(2)   otherwise, each setter does better in the secondary rather than primary role, i.e., $f_j^*(X) P_i f_i^*(X)$ and $f_i^*(X) P_i f_j^*(X)$;

(3)   the final voting outcome belongs to $C_{ij}(X)$ if and only if $f_j^*(X)$ is the secondary setter's ideal point, which in turn is true if and only if $\alpha_j \geq 90°$, where j is the secondary setter.

Point (1) follows because $F_i(X)$ and $F_j(X)$ have just one point in common, namely x^*. Point (3) is immediate. Point (2) does not apply if (1) applies and is immediate if (3) applies; otherwise, it follows from elementary trigonometry.[84]

Point (3) in Proposition 42 implies that, in two or more dimensions with a Condorcet winner x^*, the agenda setting game is often ripe for collusion. For example, Figure 18(b) shows the set of points B^* on $C_{ij}(X)$ that both setters prefer to the non-collusive outcome $f_i^*(X)$. We may also observe that

---

[83] For the reason noted in the previous footnote, $f_i(x)$ must actually lie just inside the circle.

[84] Let a be the distance from x^{i^*} to $f_j^*(X)$, let h be the distance from x^{i^*} to x^{j^*} and let a' be the distance from x^{j^*} to $f_i^*(X)$. Considering the triangle formed by the points x^{j^*}, x^{i^*} and $f_i^*(X)$, let α_i' be the angle at vertex x^{j^*}. Since $\alpha_i' < \alpha_i$, $\cos \alpha_i' > \cos \alpha_i$, i.e., $a'/h > a/h$, so $a' > a$ and, given Euclidian preferences, $f_j^*(X) P_i f_i^*(X)$. The parallel argument applies to setter j.

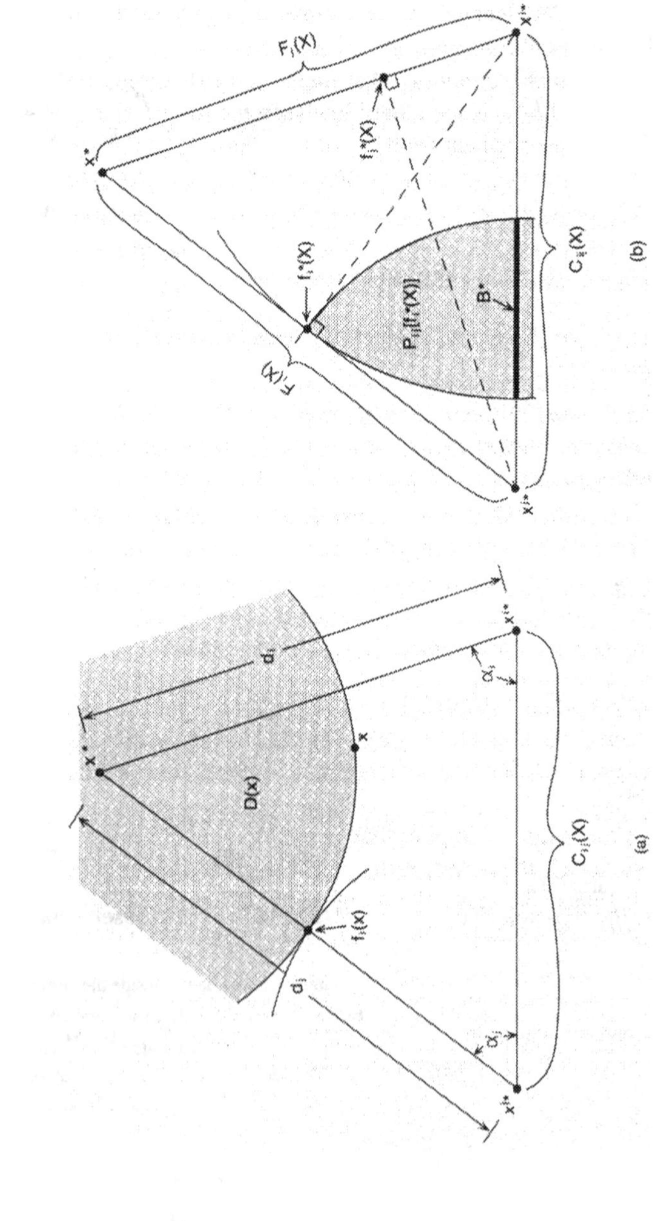

FIGURE 18 Competitive Agenda Setting in Two Dimensions with a Condorcet Winner

the *limited sequential structure* of agenda setting moves typically results in some 'tacit collusion' even in the absence of explicit collusion. Consider the situation in Figure 18(b) where setter i is primary, and suppose the agenda setters could make further proposals. We see that i can make a proposal (for example, on the $F_j(X)$ line) that lies closer to x^* than $f_i^*(X)$ does (and is therefore non-innocuous) and that, at the same time, i prefers to $f_i^*(X)$. Then j can respond in like manner, and so forth until someone proposes x^*. Limiting the setters to one proposal each, in a definite sequence, cuts short the process by which the setters would completely compete away their initial advantage.[85]

We may note that if we allow the three points x^{1^*}, x^{j^*}, and x^* to approach colinearity, then either (a) both α_i and α_j approach $0°$ (if x^* lies between x^{1^*} and x^{j^*}) so $f_i^*(X) = f_j^*(X) = x^*$ and x^* approaches $C_{ij}(X)$ or (b) either α_i or α_j (whichever setter is more 'moderate') approaches $180°$, so $f_j^*(X) = x^{i^*}$ and $f_i^*(X)$ approaches x^{i^*}, giving outcomes that parallel those for the one-dimensional case.

Given two or more dimensions, the case in which a Condorcet winner x^* exists is, of course, exceptional. In Figure 18, let us relabel the point x^* as c to designate the center of the yolk with some positive radius r. If r is very small, the previous analysis is virtually unchanged. As r increases, the set $D(x)$ — essentially the win set $P(x)$ — becomes increasingly irregular in shape.[86] Given such increasing irregularity, the maximizing behavior of the setters pulls the points $f_i^*(X)$ and $f_j^*(X)$ inward and downward until they come to rest on the $C_{ij}(X)$ line; in effect, as voter preferences become less coherent, they also have less influence on the outcome, and setter preferences become more influential.

At the extreme we can consider the 3-voter committee analyzed by Banks and Gasmi (1987). Now the third vertex of the triangle represents the ideal point of a single 'rank and file' voter who, unlike voters 1 and 2, has no agenda setting power. (Therefore, the yolk is the circle that can

[85] That i and j make their proposals in sequence is also essential for such 'tacit collusion.' If they had to make their proposals simultaneously, each in ignorance of what the other is doing, in the manner of the standard model of electoral competition, it follows that — while neither setter (with ideal point distinct from x^*) has a dominant strategy — every equilibrium pair of agenda setting strategies has at least one setter proposing x^* and gives x^* as the final voting outcome (Calvert, 1985).

[86] Bounds on this irregularity were given in 5.2 and more precise 'cardioid' bounds can be specified: see Ferejohn, McKelvey, and Packel (1984); McKelvey (1986); and Miller, Grofman, and Feld (1989).

be inscribed within the triangle and the center of the yolk is the center of the circle.)

Following Banks and Gasmi, we make the following geometrical construction, as shown in Figure 19(a). (Again we assume that x_0 is sufficiently extreme that all points in Figure 19 belong to $P(x_0)$.) We draw an arbitrary indifference curve for voter 2, such as $I_2(v)$, and the two indifference curves of voters 1 and 3 that are tangent to $I_2(v)$ and intersect at point w. Repeating this operation many times, we can trace out the locus M_2 of such intersections, extending from x^{2^*} through the point x'' on the $C_{13}(X)$ contract line.

Suppose voter 1 is the primary setter and proposes point x''. The set $D(x'')$ — essentially the win set of x'' — is shown in Figure 19(a). We see that $f_1(x'')$ is either x' (on $C_{12}(X)$) or x''' (on $C_{23}(X)$), between which voter 2 is indifferent. Suppose then that setter 1 proposes, not actually x'', but x^ϵ ever so slightly closer to x^{3^*} than x'' is; then the upper leaf of $D(x^\epsilon)$ contracts away from x^{2^*} ever so slightly and the lower leaf expands towards x^{2^*} ever so slightly, so voter 2's indifference between the closest points on the two leaves is broken in favor of the one on the $C_{12}(X)$ contract line. Essentially, $f_1(x'') = x'$. Further we can see that setter 1 in fact should propose (essentially) x'' and setter 2 should respond with (essentially) x', which will be the final voting outcome. For if 1 proposes any point x above the M_2 locus, the leaf of $D(x)$ spanning $C_{12}(X)$ pushes towards x^{2^*} and $f_1(x)$ moves away from x^{1^*}; if 1 proposes any point x below the M_2 locus, the leaf of $D(x)$ spanning $C_{23}(X)$ pushes closer to x^{2^*} than the leaf spanning $C_{12}(X)$, and $f_1(x)$ jumps away from x^{1^*}; and if 1 proposes any point x on the M_2 locus closer to (or, for that matter, further from) x^{2^*} than x'' is, both leaves of $D(x)$ spanning $C_{12}(X)$ and $C_{23}(X)$ push towards x^{2^*} and $f_1(x)$ certainly moves away from x^{1^*}. By parallel arguments, x' is also the final voting outcome if 2 is primary and 1 is secondary. Furthermore, any alternative in the set $\{x', x'', x'''\}$ may be produced as the final voting outcome by some pair of competing setters drawn out of the set $\{1, 2, 3\}$ of all voters.[87]

---

[87] We may note that $\{x', x'', x'''\}$: is the 'competitive solution' (see footnote 63) to the cooperative voting game given by Figure 19 and, as Banks and Gasmi (1987) note, the set links up with other cooperative solution concepts as well.

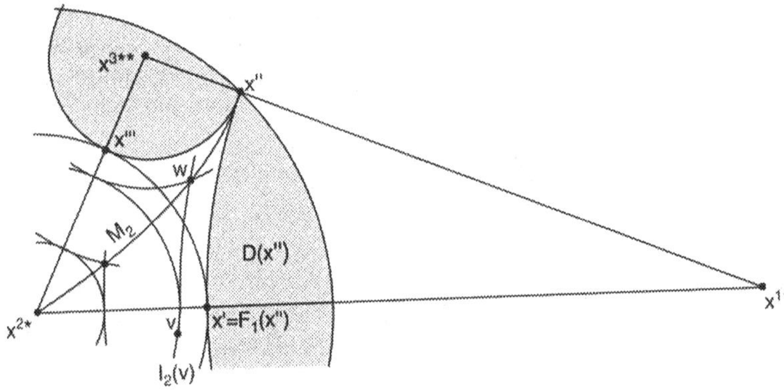

(a)

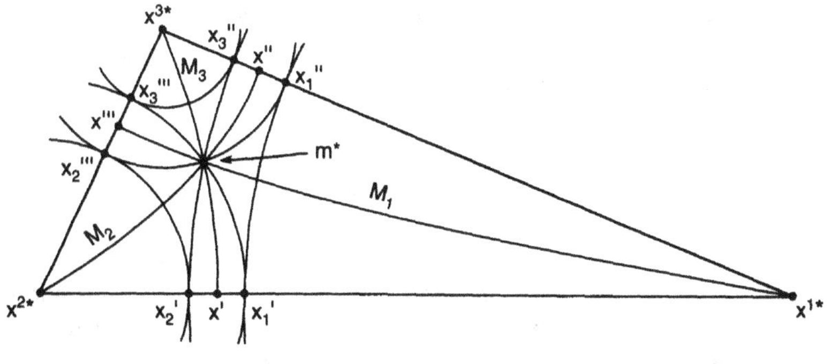

(b)

FIGURE 19 Competitive Agenda Setting in a 3-Voter Committee

8.4. Open Agenda Formation

We conclude by briefly considering certain variants of an open agenda formation process, in which the power to make proposals is widely shared. We continue to assume that, whatever the content of the agenda set A that is formed, it is a standard amendment agenda in structure and that all voting is sophisticated.

The first variant keeps us clearly within the complete information assumption that generally bounds the scope of this survey. This variant allows all committee members to make proposals in some definite order — that is, we expand the model of 2-voter competitive agenda formation discussed in the preceding subsection to one of n-voter competitive agenda formation. In principle, the same sort of backwards induction argument can be extended to any number of agenda setting moves, though clearly practical computational and analytical difficulties escalate rapidly. Banks and Gasmi (1987) in fact extend their analysis of endogenous agenda formation in a 3-voter committee to give all three voters proposal power. In this case, the final voting outcome is (more or less) centrally located and can be identified by constructing the loci M_1 and M_3 in the same manner as M_2, as shown in Figure 19(b). The three loci intersect in the common point m^*, which is in fact the final voting outcome. Banks and Gasmi show (the argument is quite complex) that, if voters make proposals in numerical order, voter 1 should propose either x_2' or x_3'', to which voter 2 should in either event respond by proposing x_1', to which voter 3's optimal response is m^*. Parallel conclusions apply if voters make proposals in other orders.

The key to the analysis described above, of course, is that voters make proposals in a definite order known to all in advance. In another and perhaps more 'open' variant of agenda formation, voters are recognized in some essentially random fashion for the purpose of making of proposals, so in this case the backward induction argument cannot be applied. Full consideration of such open agenda formation requires analytical techniques beyond the scope of this survey. But we can still reach some more limited conclusions. In particular, we can often say something about what final voting outcome will be, even if we cannot say exactly who will make what proposals; or we can put a bound on possible outcomes, even if we cannot say exactly what the outcome will be.

First, recall that when we considered the behavior of an agenda setter with gatekeeping but not monopoly proposal power, we observed that — in the event he 'opened the gates' by making a proposal — the subsequent agenda expansion process would be entirely open and, in many cases or in some measure, unpredictable. But, as we saw in 8.2, complete foresight is possible if preferences on all potential agendas are single-peaked (perhaps because of germaneness rule) or if the set X of potential proposals is sufficiently small.

More generally, partial foresight can be exercised even when complete foresight cannot be, and partial foresight may be sufficient to determine the agenda formation process and thus the final voting outcome. By way of example, Banks and Gasmi (1987) consider two further variants of endogenous agenda formation in a 3-voter committee, based on two different types of random recognition rule. In the first, chance determines which of the two other voters will have the right to make an amendment to the motion proposed by the primary agenda setter; therefore, the primary setter knows that a single subsequent proposal will be forthcoming, but he does not know which of the two other voters will be recognized to propose it. In the second, all three voters have the right to make proposals but chance determines the order in which they will be recognized; therefore, the primary setter knows that two more proposals will be forthcoming but does not know which setter will be secondary and which tertiary.

Given such circumstances, Banks and Gasmi assume that the primary setter will choose his proposal on a 'maximin' basis. Given certainty, the primary setter (say 1) can (in the manner discussed in 8.3 for the two-setter case) deduce a mapping f_1 that takes each alternative x he might propose into a final voting outcome $f_1(x)$. Given uncertainty between two possibilities — i.e., that voter 2 will make the next, or only, proposal, or that voter 3 will — primary setter 1 can deduce two different mappings f_1^2 and f_1^3 according to which uncertain contingency arises (and reflecting the different preferences of voters 2 and 3). On a 'maximin' basis, setter 1 can then combine f_1^2 and f_1^3 into a single mapping f_1 such that $f_1(x) = f_1^2(x)$ if $f_1^3(x)R_1f_1^2(x)$ and $f_1(x) = f_1^3(x)$ if $f_1^2(x)R_1f_1^3(x)$.

Banks and Gasmi then show that, in the first case, uncertainty about who will have the right to make the second proposal induces the primary setter (whoever he is, but let us suppose voter 1) to make the 'moderate' proposal m^*. (Recall that if primary setter 1 knows that voter 2, say, will make the second and only other proposal, he will make the relatively 'immoderate' proposal x'' along the $C_{13}(X)$ contract line.) This in turn induces the secondary setter (whoever he turns out to be) to propose the point on his contract line with 1 such that 1 ever so slightly prefers that point to m^*. In Figure 19(b), for example, if 1 is primary and 2 turns out to be secondary, 2 proposes a point slightly closer to x^{1^*} than x_2' on $C_{12}(X)$, where $x_2' I_1 m^*$. Thus the final voting outcome is (essentially) x_2'. Note that primary setter 1's maximin proposal strategy leaves 1 indifferent as to who the secondary setter actually turns out to be, since, if it had been 3 instead of 2, 3 would have proposed (essentially) x_3'', and $x_3'' I_1 m^* I_1 x_2'$. Note also that primary setter 1 has suffered a (relatively small) loss, appropriated by the secondary setter, as a result of his uncertainty as to who the secondary setter will be, since (as we saw in 8.3) x' is the outcome in the event 1 knows 2 is secondary and x_2' lies somewhat further from x^{1^*}, and closer to x^{2^*}, than x' does. Obviously, parallel arguments apply to 2 and 3 as primary setters.

Finally, we consider the case in which all three voters have the right to make proposals, but the primary setter — though he knows two more proposals will be forthcoming — does not know the order in which they will be made. In this case, Banks and Gasmi show that the final voting outcome is m^*, regardless of the order in which the proposals are actually made. This result follows directly from the three-setter case with certainty discussed at the outset of this subsection, since we saw there that primary setter 1 might propose either x_2' or x_3'' if 2 were the secondary setter, and by parallel considerations, he would do the same if 3 were secondary. Thus in fact the primary setter does not need to know who is secondary and who tertiary, and uncertainty on this score does not affect his behavior. And of course there can be no uncertainty for the secondary or tertiary setter. Thus the outcome is the same as in the certainty case.

The kind of calculations on which Banks and Gasmi base their conclusions would seem to become excessively formidable in a larger committee. But even in this case we can put significant bounds on final voting outcome resulting from open agenda formation. Consider an open agenda formation process of the following nature. The status quo x_0 is automatically on the agenda. Any voter is free to seek recognition and propose other alternatives to add to the agenda. In this way, a standard amendment agenda is built backwards until no further proposals are made. At this point the agenda is fixed and voting takes place in a sophisticated fashion. At the agenda formation stage, voters know that voting will be sophisticated and know majority preference over all alternatives, but they do not know who will subsequently be recognized to make proposals or what proposals they will make.

However the agenda A is formed, we know from Proposition 16 that the final voting outcome will belong to $B(A)$ and, more specifically (from Proposition 25), that it will belong to $B(A:x_0)$. But we can have more precise expectations. At some point in the agenda formation process, an *equilibrium agenda* may be reached in that no voter can make any further proposal that can change the final outcome in a way he prefers.[88] At such a point of equilibrium, we may expect no further proposals to be forthcoming. Of course, if the alternative space X is infinite, we have in general no assurance that equilibrium will ever be reached. This is especially likely to be true if the agenda is manipulable. But we have seen from Proposition 36 that a standard amendment agenda is immune to manipulation if voting is sophisticated. Moreover, the same proposition specifies the condition necessary and sufficient for such an agenda A to be invulnerable to expansion. It is immediate that invulnerability to expansion is sufficient for agenda equilibrium, and it should be clear that it is necessary as well. For A is vulnerable to expansion only if there is some x'' in X that beats the alternative x' that would the voting outcome from A. Therefore, if an agenda is vulnerable to expansion, some voter — indeed a majority of voters — has an incentive to expand it. Thus the condition for A to be an equilibrium agenda is equivalent to the condition for A to be invulnerable to expansion: namely, that A — and, more particularly, the chain of non-innocuous proposals in A — be externally stable in X. This in turn is equivalent to saying that x', the voting outcome from the equilibrium agenda, belongs to $B(X)$ and, more particularly, to $B(X:x_0)$. Since $B(X)$ is a subset of $UC(X)$ it follows that the voting outcome is Pareto-optimal and, in the spatial case, more or less centrally located.[89]

---

[88] This usage borrows from Ferejohn, Fiorina, and McKelvey (1987). The following discussion draws on Miller, Grofman, and Feld (1990a).

[89] In assuming that an equilibrium agenda will be reached, we have assumed that, so long as non-innocuous alternatives remain to be proposed, they will be added to the agenda. It is plausible also to expect that *only* non-innocuous alternatives will be proposed, since innocuous proposals are futile. It is not necessary for the latter to be true to reach the conclusion that the final voting outcomes belongs to $B(X:x_0)$. (That is, even if voters add innocuous alternatives to the agenda — perhaps for reasons of 'position taking' — the voting outcome is unchanged.) However, if only non-innocuous alternatives are proposed, it may be checked that, in the resulting standard amendment agenda, the sophisticated equivalent $s(v)$ at every decision node v is always identical to the challenged alternative $\Gamma'(v)$, which implies the sincere and sophisticated voting strategies of all voters coincide. Thus, though we assume sophisticated voting, such voting is observationally equivalent to sincere voting. This was first noted by Austen-Smith (1987), who characterized such voting as 'sophisticated sincerity' (also

In most cases, $B(X:x_0)$ is a multi-element set, so there is some indeterminacy in the overall agenda formation process — the final outcome depends in part on who is recognized in what order and what proposals they make. But in some cases, $B(X:x_0)$ is a one-element set, in which case such factors cannot influence the final outcome, which accordingly can be fully foreseen. One obvious sufficient condition is that there is a Condorcet winner x^* in X, so that $B(X) = B(X:x_0) = \{x^*\}$. (This formalizes the analysis in 8.2 concerning gatekeeping under a germaneness rule inducing unidimensionality.) And $B(X:x_0)$ is likely to be a one-element set if X is a sufficiently small finite set. (Another example in 8.2 illustrated this.) But $B(X:x_0)$ can be a one-element set even if there is no Condorcet winner and X is large. This will be true whenever there is some alternative x in $P(x_0)$ such that the pair $\{x, x_0\}$ is externally stable in X or, putting the matter more intuitively, such that x is the Condorcet winner in $P(x_0)$. Ferejohn, Fiorina, and McKelvey (1987) note a prominent example in the context of distributive politics (recall 3.5). The null project package $< 0, \dots , 0 >$ beats every package that provides projects for only a minority of voters; the package that provides the cheapest $(n + 1)/2$ projects beats all other packages that provide projects for a majority of voters, so this pair of alternatives is externally stable in X. Thus, given sophisticated voting and any standard agenda with the null package as the status quo, once the cheapest majority package is proposed, an equilibrium agenda is reached. Moreover, there is no other equilibrium agenda. So, even though we cannot know who will propose what, we can foresee the final outcome.

Finally, considering a result given by McKelvey (1986), we can allow for an even greater degree of openness in agenda formation and still put definite bounds on final outcomes. Suppose that agenda formation takes place as described above, but that the order in which proposals are made does not determine their position in the voting order. When all alternatives forming the agenda set A have been proposed, they are placed in some random or otherwise unpredictable order for voting under a standard amendment agenda. Only once voting begins do voters know the particular structure of the agenda and then voting is sophisticated. Of course the voting outcome belongs to $B(A)$, a subset of $UC(A)$.[90] We may note that, if x belongs

---

see footnote 51) and who noted that this fact may help account for the difficulty in documenting instances of sophisticated voting in actual legislatures.

[90] If the status quo x_0 is automatically on the agenda *and last in the voting order*, the final

to $UC(X)$, x also belongs to $UC(A)$ for any subset A of X that includes x. Suppose alternative z has been proposed, alternative x has not been proposed, and x covers z. If x is then added to the agenda, then — regardless where x or z may end up in the voting order and regardless of what other proposals have been and may yet be proposed — z is eliminated as a possible final voting outcome. McKelvey shows that this implies that all voters may as well restrict their proposals to alternatives in $UC(X)$. From this, it follows, of course, that the final voting outcome must itself belong to $UC(X)$. Even if proposals are made without any kind of strategic calculation (e.g., sincerely) and, as a result, alternatives outside of $UC(X)$ are proposed, it is likely (though not certain) that they will also be covered in A and accordingly precluded as possible outcomes. Thus, even given the most open type of agenda formation, voting outcomes are likely to be constrained in a reasonable way.[91]

9. CONCLUSION

This essay has surveyed the theory of committee voting pioneered by Duncan Black and advanced by Robin Farquharson. It is fair to say that, within the framework established by Black and Farquharson, the theory of committee voting is now largely complete and most of its results have been covered here. The major gap lies in the area of agenda formation processes. Even here important progress has been made, but a decisive and complete treatment requires consideration of procedural and institutional details beyond the scope of the original Black–Farquharson formulation. And a more general treatment of committee voting needs to go beyond the Black–Farquharson framework by taking account of the environment of incomplete information

---

voting outcome belongs to $B(A:x_0)$. McKelvey's (1986) discussion does not provide for a distinguished status quo alternative.

[91] Actual legislative bodies are rarely as freewheeling as this discussion suggests, and more detailed aspects of parliamentary procedure (e.g., recognition rules, motions to 'move the previous question' or otherwise shut off new proposals, reconsideration votes, and repeated voting sessions), in addition to more complex institutional structures, may further constrain voting outcomes. Moreover, seemingly small changes in such procedures (and institutions) may have rather large effects on outcomes. For treatments along these lines, see Ferejohn, Fiorina, and McKelvey (1987) and Baron and Ferejohn (1989a and 1989b). A principal theme of Baron and Ferejohn (1989a) is the advantage that may accrue to the voter making the first proposal; this theme is supported by remarks made above in 8.2 concerning the proposal power of a gatekeeping agenda setter in the absence of a Condorcet winner.

in which committee members typically operate. Other monographs in this series (Calvert, 1986; Banks, 1991) begin this task.

References

Arrow, K.A. (1951). *Social Choice and Individual Values*. New York: Wiley.

Austen-Smith, D. (1987). 'Sophisticated Sincerity: Voting Over Endogenous Agendas,' *American Political Science Review*, **81**, 1323–1330.

Banks, J.S. (1985). 'Sophisticated Voting Outcomes and Agenda Control,' *Social Choice and Welfare*, **1**, 295–306.

Banks, J.S. (1989). 'Equilibrium Outcomes in Two-Stage Amendment Procedures,' *American Journal of Political Science*, **33**, 25–43.

Banks, J.S. (1990). 'Monopoly Agenda Control with Asymmetric Information,' *Quarterly Journal of Economics*, **105**, 455–464.

Banks, J.S. (1991). *Signaling Games in Political Science*. Chur: Harwood Academic Publishers.

Banks, J.S. (1993). 'Two-sided Uncertainty in the Monopoly Agenda Setter Model', *Journal of Public Economics*, **50**, 429–444.

Banks, J.S., and F. Gasmi (1987). 'Endogenous Agenda Formation in Three-Person Committees,' *Social Choice and Welfare*, **4**, 133–152.

Baron, D.P., and J.A. Ferejohn (1989a). 'The Power to Propose,' in *Models of Strategic Choice in Politics*, ed. by P.C. Ordeshook. Ann Arbor: University of Michigan Press.

Baron, D.P., and J.A. Ferejohn (1989b). 'Bargaining in Legislatures.' *American Political Science Review*, **83**, 1181–1206.

Bernholz, P. (1972). 'Logrolling, Arrow-Paradox and Cyclical Majorities,' *Public Choice* **15**, 87–95.

Bernholz, P. (1974). 'Logrolling, Arrow-Paradox and Decision Rules: A Generalization,' *Kyklos*, **27**, 49–62.

Bjurulf, B.H., and R.G. Niemi (1982). 'Order-of-Voting Effects,' in *Power, Voting, and Voting Power*, ed. by M.J. Holler. Wurzburg: Physica-Verlag.

Black, D. (1948). 'On the Rationale of Group Decision-Making,' *Journal of Political Economy*, **56**, 23–34.

Black, D. (1958). *The Theory of Committees and Elections*. Cambridge: Cambridge University Press.

Bordes, G. (1983). 'On the Possibility of Reasonable Consistent Majoritarian Choice: Some Positive Results,' *Journal of Economic Theory*, **31**, 122–132.

Calvert, R.L. (1985). 'Robustness of the Multidimensional Voting Model: Candidate Motivations, Uncertainty, and Convergence,' *American Journal of Political Science*, **29**, 69–95.

Calvert, R.L. (1986). *Models of Imperfect Information in Politics*. Chur: Harwood Academic Publishers.

Craven, J. (1971). 'Majority Voting and Social Choice,' *Review of Economic Studies*, **38**, 265–267.

Davis, O., and M. Hinich (1966). 'A Mathematical Model of Policy Formation in A Democratic Society,' in *Mathematical Applications in Political Science*, II, ed. by J. Bernd. Dallas: Southern Methodist University Press.

Denzau, A.T., and R.J. Mackay (1983). 'Gatekeeping and Monopoly Power of Committees: An Analysis of Sincere and Sophisticated Behavior,' *American Journal of Political Science*, **27**, 739–761.

Downs, A. (1957). *An Economic Theory of Democracy*. New York: Harper & Row.

Dummett, M. (1984). *Voting Procedures*. Oxford: Oxford University Press.

Dummett, M., and R. Farquharson (1961). 'Stability in Voting,' *Econometrica*, **29**, 33–42.

Dutta, B. (1988). 'Covering Sets and a New Condorcet Choice Correspondence,' *Journal of Economic Theory*, **44**, 63–80.

Dutta B. (1990). 'On the Tournament Equilibrium Set,' *Social Choice and Welfare*, **7**, 381–383.

Epstein, D.L. (1992). 'Uncovering Some Subtleties of the Uncovered Set.' Unpublished paper, Department of Political Science, Columbia University.

Farquharson, R. (1956a). 'Straightforwardness in Voting Procedures,' *Oxford Economic Papers* (New Series), **8**, 80–89.

Farquharson, R. (1956b). 'Strategic Information in Games and in Voting,' in *Information Theory*, ed. by C. Cherry. London: Butterworths.

Farquharson, R. (1966). 'The Application of Game Theory to Committee Procedure,' in *Operational Research and the Social Sciences*, ed. by J.R. Lawrence. London: Tavistock Publications.

Farquharson, R. (1969a). *Theory of Voting*. New Haven. Yale University Press.

Farquharson, R. (1969b). 'Sophisticated Voting and an Example due to M. Kreweras,' in *La Décision: Aggrégation et Dynamique des Ordres de Préférence*, ed. by G. Guilbaud. Paris: Editions du Centre Nationale de la Recherche Scientifique.

Feld, S.L., B. Grofman and N.R. Miller (1988). 'Centripetal Forces in Spatial Voting Games: On the Size of the Yolk,' *Public Choice*, **59**, 37–50.

Feld, S.L., B. Grofman and N.R. Miller (1989). 'Limits on Agenda Control in Spatial Voting Games,' *Mathematical and Computer Modelling*, **12**, 405–416.

Feld, S.L., B. Grofman, R. Hartley, M. Kilgour and N.R. Miller (1987). 'The Uncovered Set in Spatial Voting Games,' *Theory and Decision*, **23**, 129–155.

Ferejohn, J.A. (March, 1975). 'Sophisticated Voting with Separable Preferences.' Social Science Working Paper No. 77, California Institute of Technology.

Ferejohn, J.A., and D.M. Grether (1974). 'On a Class of Rational Social Decision Procedures,' *Journal of Economic Theory*, **8**, 471–482.

Ferejohn, J.A., M. Fiorina and R.D. McKelvey (1987). 'Sophisticated Voting and Agenda Independence in the Distributive Politics Setting,' *American Journal of Political Science*, **31**, 169–193.

Ferejohn, J.A., R.D. McKelvey and E.W. Packel (1984). 'Limiting Distributions for Continuous State Markov Voting Models,' *Social Choice and Welfare*, **1**, 45–67.

Fiorina, M.P. (1981). 'Universalism, Reciprocity, and Distributive Policy Making in Majority Rule Institutions,' in *Research in Public Policy Analysis and Management*, ed. by J.P. Crecine. Greenwich: JAI Press.

Fishburn, P.C. (1973). *The Theory of Social Choice*. Princeton: Princeton University Press.

Gibbard, A. (1973). 'Manipulation of Voting Schemes: A General Result,' *Econometrica*, 41, 587–601.

Gretlein, R.J. (1983). 'Dominance Elimination Procedures on Finite Alternative Games,' *International Journal of Game Theory*, 12, 107–113.

Grofman, B. (1969). 'Some Notes on Voting Schemes and the Will of the Majority.' *Public Choice*, 7, 65–80.

Harary, F., R.Z. Norman and D. Cartwright (1965). *Structural Models: An Introduction to the Theory of Directed Graphs*. New York: Wiley.

Hartley, R., and D.M. Kilgour (1987). 'The Geometry of the Uncovered Set,' *Mathematical Social Sciences*, 14, 175–183.

Ingberman, D.E., and D.A. Yao (1991). 'Circumventing Formal Structure Through Commitment: Presidential Influence and Agenda Control,' *Public Choice*, 70, 151–179.

Jung, J.P. (1990). 'Black and Farquharson on Order-of-Voting Effects: An Extension,' *Social Choice and Welfare*, 7, 319–331.

Kadane, J.B. (1972). 'On Division of The Question,' *Public Choice*, 13, 47–54.

Koehler, D.H. (1975). 'Vote Trading and the Voting Paradox: A Proof of Logical Equivalence,' *American Political Science Review*, 69, 954–960.

Kramer, G.H. (1972). 'Sophisticated Voting Over Multidimensional Choice Spaces,' *Journal of Mathematical Sociology*, 2, 165–180.

Kramer, G.H. (1977). 'Some Procedural Aspects of Majority Rule,' in *Due Process*, ed. by J.R. Pennock and J.W. Chapman. New York: New York University Press.

Krehbiel, K. (1985). 'Obstruction and Representativeness in Legislatures,' *American Journal of Political Science*, 29, 643–659.

Krehbiel, K. (1987). 'Sophisticated Committees and Structure-Induced Equilibria in Congress,' in *Congress: Structure and Policy*, ed. by M.D. McCubbins and T. Sullivan. Cambridge: Cambridge University Press.

Mackay, R.J., and C.L. Weaver (1983). 'Commodity Bundling and Agenda Control in the Public Sector,' *Quarterly Journal of Economics*, 98, 611–635.

May, K.O. (1952). 'A Set of Independent Necessary and Sufficient Conditions for Simple Majority Decision,' *Econometrica*, 20, 680–684.

McGarvey, D. (1953). 'A Theorem on the Construction of Voting Paradoxes,' *Econometrica*, 21, 608–610.

McKelvey, R.D. (1976). 'Intransitivities in Multidimensional Voting Models and Some Implications for Agenda Control,' *Journal of Economic Theory*, 12, 472–482.

McKelvey, R.D. (1979). 'General Conditions For Global Intransitivities in Formal Voting Models,' *Econometrica*, 47, 1085–1112.

McKelvey, R.D. (1981). 'A Theory of Optimal Agenda Design,' *Management Science*, 27, 303–321.

McKelvey, R.D. (1986). 'Covering, Dominance, and Institution Free Properties of Social Choice,' *American Journal of Political Science*, **30**, 283–314.

McKelvey, R.D., and R.G. Niemi (1978). 'A Multistage Game Representation of Sophisticated Voting for Binary Procedures,' *Journal of Economic Theory*, **18**, 1–22.

McKelvey, R.D., P.C. Ordeshook and M.A. Winer (1978). 'The Competitive Solution for *N*-Person Games without Transferable Utility, with an Application to Committee Games,' *American Political Science Review*, **72**, 599–615.

Miller, N.R. (1975). 'Logrolling and the Arrow Paradox: A Note,' *Public Choice*, **21**, 107–110.

Miller, N.R. (1977a). 'Logrolling, Vote Trading, and the Paradox of Voting: A Game-Theoretical Overview,' *Public Choice*, **30**, 51–75.

Miller, N.R. (1977b). 'Graph-Theoretical Approaches to the Theory of Voting,' *American Journal of Political Science*, **21**, 769–803.

Miller, N.R. (1980). 'A New Solution Set for Tournaments and Majority Voting,' *American Journal of Political Science*, **24**, 68–96.

Miller, N.R. (1982). 'The Complete Structure of Majority Rule on Distributive Politics.' Paper presented to the Annual Meeting of the Public Choice Society, San Antonio, Texas.

Miller, N.R. (1983). 'The Covering Relation in Tournaments: Two Corrections,' *American Journal of Political Science*, **27**, 382–385.

Miller, N.R. (1986). 'Competing Agenda Setters with Policy Preferences.' Paper presented at the Hoover Institution Conference on The Political Economy of Institutions.

Miller, N.R., B. Grofman and S.L. Feld (1989). 'The Geometry of Majority Rule,' *Journal of Theoretical Politics*, **1**, 379–406.

Miller, N.R., B. Grofman and S.L. Feld (1990a). 'Cycle Avoiding Trajectories, Strategic Agendas, and the Duality of Memory and Foresight: An Informal Exposition,' *Public Choice*, **64**, 265–278.

Miller, N.R., B. Grofman and S.L. Feld (1990b). 'The Structure of the Banks Set,' *Public Choice*, **66**, 243–251.

Moulin, H. (1979). 'Dominance-solvable Voting Schemes,' *Econometrica*, **47**, 1337–1351.

Moulin, H. (1986). 'Choosing From a Tournament,' *Social Choice and Welfare*, **3**, 271–291.

Niemi, R.G. (1983). 'An Exegesis of Farquharson's *Theory of Voting*,' *Public Choice*, **40**, 323–328.

Niemi, R.G., and R.J. Gretlein (1985). 'A Precise Restatement and Extension of Black's Theorem on Voting Orders,' *Public Choice*, **47**, 371–376.

Niemi, R.G., and B.E. Rasch (1987). 'An Extension of Black's Theorem on Voting Orders to the Successive Procedure,' *Public Choice*, **54**, 187–190.

Niskanen, W. (1971). *Bureaucracy and Representative Government*. Chicago: Aldine-Atherton.

Oppenheimer, J.A. (1972). 'Relating Coalitions of Minorities to the Voters' Paradox or Putting Fly in the Democratic Pie.' Paper presented to Annual Meeting of Southwest Political Science Association, San Antonio, Texas.

Ordeshook, P.C., and T. Schwartz (1987). 'Agendas and the Control of Political Outcomes,' *American Political Science Review*, **81**, 179–199.

Plott, C.R., and M. Levine (1976). 'A Model of Agenda Influence on Committee Decisions,' *American Economic Review*, **68**, 146–160.

Rasch, B.E. (1987). 'Manipulation and Strategic Voting in the Norwegian Parliament,' *Public Choice*, **52**, 57–73.

Reid, K.B. (1991a). 'Majority Tournaments: Sincere and Sophisticated Voting Decisions under Amendment Procedure.' *Mathematical Social Sciences*, **21**, 1–19.

Reid, K.B. (1991b). 'The Relationship Between Two Algorithms for Decisions Via Sophisticated Majority Voting with an Agenda.' *Discrete Applied Mathematics*, **31**, 23–28.

Romer, T., and H. Rosenthal (1978). 'Political Resource Allocation, Controlled Agendas, and the Status Quo,' *Public Choice*, **33/4**, 27–45.

Romer, T., and H. Rosenthal (1979). 'Bureaucrats vs. Voters: On the Political Economy of Resource Allocation by Direct Democracy,' *Quarterly Journal of Economics*, **93**, 563–588.

Rosenthal, H. (1990). 'The Setter Model,' in *Advances in the Spatial Theory of Voting*, ed. by J. Enelow and M. Hinich. Cambridge: Cambridge University Press.

Schwartz, T. (1977). 'Collective Choice, Separation of Issues, and Vote Trading,' *American Political Science Review*, **71**, 999–1010.

Schwartz, T. (1986). *The Logic of Collective Choice*. New York: Columbia University Press.

Schwartz, T. (1990). 'Cyclic Tournaments and Cooperative Majority Voting: A Solution.' *Social Choice and Welfare*, **7**, 19–29.

Shepsle, K.A. (1979). 'Institutional Arrangements and Equilibrium in Multidimensional Voting Models,' *American Journal of Political Science*, **23**, 27–59.

Shepsle, K.A., and B.R. Weingast (1981). 'Political Preferences for the Pork Barrel: A Generalization,' *American Journal of Political Science*, **25**, 96–111.

Shepsle, K.A., and B.R. Weingast (1984a). 'Uncovered Sets and Sophisticated Voting Outcomes with Implications for Agenda Institutions,' *American Journal of Political Science*, **28**, 49–74.

Shepsle, K.A., and B.R. Weingast (1984b). 'When Do Rules of Procedure Matter?' *Journal of Politics*, **46**, 206–221.

Tovey, C.A. (1992). 'The Almost Surely Shrinking Yolk,' Political Economy Working Paper No. 161, School of Business and Center in Political Economy, Washington University.

Ward, B. (1961). 'Majority Rule and Allocation,' *Journal of Conflict Resolution*, **5**, 379–389.

Weingast, B.R. (1979). 'A Rational Choice Perspective on Congressional Norms,' *American Journal of Political Science*, **23**, 245–262.

Weingast, B.R. (1989). 'Floor Behavior in the U.S. Congress: Committee Power under the Open Rule,' *American Political Science Review*, **83**, 795–815.

Wilson, R. (1986). 'Forward and Backward Agenda Procedures: Committee Experiments on Structurally Induced Equilibrium,' *Journal of Politics*, **48**, 390–409.

Index

FUNDAMENTALS OF PURE AND APPLIED ECONOMICS

SECTIONS AND EDITORS

BALANCE OF PAYMENTS AND INTERNATIONAL FINANCE
W. Branson, Princeton University
DISTRIBUTION
A. Atkinson, London School of Economics
ECONOMIC DEVELOPMENT STUDIES
S. Chakravarty, Delhi School of Economics
ECONOMIC HISTORY
P. David, Stanford University, and M. Lévy-Leboyer, Université Paris X
ECONOMIC SYSTEMS
J. M. Montias, Yale University
ECONOMICS OF HEALTH, EDUCATION, POVERTY AND CRIME
V. Fuchs, Stanford University
ECONOMICS OF THE HOUSEHOLD AND INDIVIDUAL BEHAVIOR
J. Muellbauer, University of Oxford
ECONOMICS OF TECHNOLOGICAL CHANGE
F. M. Scherer, Harvard University
EVOLUTION OF ECONOMIC STRUCTURES, LONG-TERM MODELS,
PLANNING POLICY, INTERNATIONAL ECONOMIC STRUCTURES
W. Michalski, O.E.C.D., Paris
EXPERIMENTAL ECONOMICS
C. Plott, California Institute of Technology
GOVERNMENT OWNERSHIP AND REGULATION OF ECONOMIC
ACTIVITY
E. Bailey, Carnegie-Mellon University, USA
INTERNATIONAL ECONOMIC ISSUES
B. Balassa, The World Bank
INTERNATIONAL TRADE
M. Kemp, University of New South Wales
LABOR AND ECONOMICS
F. Welch, Texas A & M University, Texas, USA
MACROECONOMIC THEORY
J. Grandmont, CEPREMAP, Paris
MARXIAN ECONOMICS
J. Roemer, University of California, Davis
NATURAL RESOURCES AND ENVIRONMENTAL ECONOMICS
C. Henry, Ecole Polytechnique, Paris

ORGANIZATION THEORY AND ALLOCATION PROCESSES
A. Postlewaite, University of Pennsylvania
POLITICAL SCIENCE AND ECONOMICS
J. Ferejohn, Stanford University
PROGRAMMING METHODS IN ECONOMICS
M. Balinski, Ecole Polytechnique, Paris
PUBLIC EXPENDITURES
P. Dasgupta, University of Cambridge
REGIONAL AND URBAN ECONOMICS
R. Arnott, Boston College, Massachusetts
SOCIAL CHOICE THEORY
A. Sen, Harvard University
STOCHASTIC METHODS IN ECONOMIC ANALYSIS
Editor to be announced
TAXES
R. Guesnerie, Ecole des Hautes Etudes en Sciences Sociales, Paris
THEORY OF THE FIRM AND INDUSTRIAL ORGANIZATION
A. Jacquemin, Université Catholique de Louvain

FUNDAMENTALS OF PURE
AND APPLIED ECONOMICS
PUBLISHED TITLES

For Product Safety Concerns and Information please contact our EU
representative GPSR@taylorandfrancis.com
Taylor & Francis Verlag GmbH, Kaufingerstraße 24, 80331 München, Germany